THE
LITTLE BOOK
OF
Object-Oriented
Programming

HENRY F. LEDGARD

Prentice Hall, Englewood Cliffs, New Jersey 07632

Library of Congress Cataloging-in-Publication Data

The little book of object-oriented programming / Henry Ledgard.
      p.   cm.
    Includes bibliographical references and index.
    ISBN 0-13-396342-X
    1. Object-oriented programming (Computer science). I. Title.
QA76.64.L44   1996
005.13—dc20

                            95-22671
                            CIP

Publisher: Alan Apt
Production Editor: Mona Pompili
Cover Designer: Bruce Kenselaar
Manufacturing Buyer: Donna Sullivan
Editorial Assistant: Shirley McGuire

© 1996 by Prentice-Hall, Inc.
Simon & Schuster/A Viacom Company
Upper Saddle River, New Jersey 07458

The author and publisher of this book have used their best efforts in preparing this book. These efforts include the development, research, and testing of the theories and programs to determine their effectiveness. The author and publisher shall not be liable in any event for incidental or consequential damages in connection with, or arising out of, the furnishing, performance, or use of these programs.

Printed in the United States of America

10 9 8 7 6 5 4 3 2 1

ISBN   0-13-396342-X

PRENTICE-HALL INTERNATIONAL (UK) LIMITED, *London*
PRENTICE-HALL OF AUSTRALIA PTY. LIMITED, *Sydney*
PRENTICE-HALL CANADA, INC., *Toronto*
PRENTICE-HALL HISPANOAMERICANA, S.A., *Mexico*
PRENTICE-HALL OF INDIA PRIVATE LIMITED, *New Delhi*
PRENTICE-HALL OF JAPAN, INC., *Tokyo*
SIMON & SCHUSTER ASIA PTE. LTD., *Singapore*
EDITORA PRENTICE-HALL DO BRASIL, LTDA., *Rio de Janeiro*

*Dedicated to Bernie V Falk, M.A.,
a wonderful man,
who is brilliant, kind, and
deserving of several Nobel prizes.*

Preface

This book offers a simple presentation of object-oriented programming. It is based on the premise that there is much confusion about OOP. Many programs are claimed to be object-oriented but are not really different from those of yesteryear. Many programmers think they understand object-oriented programming but do not. Many non-programmers are held hostage to the OOP mystique.

The book starts from an elementary programming base and builds on this base to unfold the essence of OOP. Object-oriented programming is developed in stages. Each stage presents a single key principle. The book concludes with a program of some substance, a program for a card game called Flash.

The book makes use of a series of mini-languages. The mini-languages are based on familiar notation and represent a tiny fragment of real languages. Thus, we can introduce OOP with a minimum of notation and without the distractions of the full syntax of a particular language.

This book is written for the following:

1. Pascal and Ada programmers who want to understand the essence of the object-oriented paradigm.

2. C programmers and C++ programmers who have started to learn object-oriented programming and want to go deeper.

3. Fortran, Basic, and Cobol programmers who wonder what object-oriented programming is truly about.

4. Computer programmers who are a bit afraid of object-oriented programming because they do not really understand it.

5. Anyone who wants a clear explanation of the truly fundamental issues in the field.

The book features a number of multiple-choice questions.

This book has gained a great deal from students in the Survey of Programming Languages course at the University of Toledo. Amit Kolhatkar spent many hours kindly and skillfully helping to prepare this manuscript. This book is a derivative work based on an earlier book, *Programming Language Landscape*, Second Edition, written by Michael Marcotty and Henry Ledgard.

Henry F. Ledgard

Contents

CHAPTER 1

Introduction

This book is an introduction to object-oriented programming. Questions arise. What is object-oriented programming, really? Is it any good? Is it really good? Is it difficult? How will one know it when one sees it? Is object-oriented programming a single thing, or does it come in stages? These are not easy questions.

Object-oriented programming is a complex topic. It has become a field of its own. It is not easy to find and understand the key concepts in this area. There is a rather significant vocabulary around the area that can make the field appear difficult. And there is a set of programming languages that are used and that may be unfamiliar. This can make the field appear overwhelming.

We present object-oriented programming through a series of mini-languages. The first is based on *types*. This is a fundamental notion for object-oriented programming. A type denotes a kind of "noun," and object-oriented programming is about nouns or things rather than verbs. That is where the word "object" comes in.

The next mini-language is about *type definitions*. A type definition is a means of defining new kinds of types, or, if you will, new kinds of objects. A programming language has a fixed number of built-in types, and a type definition is a way of introducing new kinds of objects that are more related to an application at hand.

The next step is related to programming languages in general. To define a new type we usually need to define what kinds of actions we can do with the new kinds of objects. If our type, for example, is a deck of cards, we need to define what shuffling means and what dealing means. These "operations" go with the type. To write an object-oriented program, we need

1

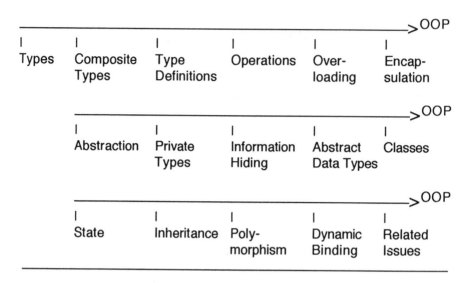

Figure 1.1   A Systematic Presentation of OOP.

to group everything about a new type together. This grouping idea gives rise to the next mini-language, which is about *modules* or *packages*.

The fourth step is a bit technical. We would like to be able to say that a given section of a program defines everything about a type. We would also like to be able to define as many objects of the type as we want. This means we would like to have a special kind of program unit just for objects of a given type. This idea leads us to the fourth mini-language, which is about *modules that represent objects*.

Dealing with growth and change is a major issue in programming. With object-oriented programming it is important to be able to extend a program in a convenient fashion. This leads to a issue directly related to object-oriented programming, *inheritance*. This is the topic of the fifth mini-language. Inheritance is a key issue in reusing and adapting existing software.

The subject of object-oriented programming can be viewed as a series of ideas that relate to a certain approach to programming. We do *not* need to have these these ideas explicitly in a language to achieve object-oriented programming. These ideas follow in a somewhat natural progression and can be presented in order as illustrated in Figure 1.1.

We attempt to convey object-oriented programming in its essence, not necessarily linked to a particular programming language.

CHAPTER 2

Types

The main theme of this chapter, and the rest of this book is that the OOP paradigm is a better mechanism for software engineering and a paradigm which greatly improves productivity and software maintenance.

[Bindu Rao, 1992]

$\mathcal{A}$ program is useful because it models a real-world process. To do this, it uses program objects that represent real-world objects. The closer the properties of a program object mirror those of the corresponding real-world object, the more effective will be the program and the easier it will be to understand.

Early programming languages permitted only numbers as objects; everything had to be represented by numbers. Because early programming was largely computational, the mapping between real objects and program objects was generally simple, though by no means perfect. With improvements in the design of programming languages, much more varied and useful kinds of objects have been allowed, leading eventually to object-oriented programming.

We begin our discussion of object-oriented programming with the notion of *type*. In its simple and most primitive form, object-oriented programming is about types. In particular, object-oriented programming takes the perspective of programming around nouns, or things. The things are called "objects." Some examples of objects are

3

```
3
81
A circle of radius 4
A deck of cards
A checkerboard
This book
```

Rather than use the word "type," the word "class" is often used in object-oriented programming. The terms "type" and "class" can, for the most part, be considered synonymous. We may view object-oriented programming simply as programming where types are the central issue in the construction of the program.

We will see as our chapters progress, that object-oriented programming is, in a way, a series of generalizations related to the concept of elementary types.

We now define a few terms related to object-oriented programming:

Type   A set of objects and the operations on the objects.

Composite type A type whose values have components.

Class   A type.

Instance   An object, i.e., a member of a class or type.

Overloading   The use of the same operator with different types of arguments. The operator has different meanings according to the types of its operands.

In this chapter, we discuss the kinds of types that can be an intrinsic part of languages. These are the *primitive types* of a language. In the next chapter, we take up the issue again with a discussion of techniques that allow the programmer to specify new data types that more closely match the real objects of a given problem.

2.1   MINI-LANGUAGE TYPE

The context-free syntax of Mini-language Type is given in Figure 2.1. Note here that the symbol *b* represents the single blank character.

Figure 2.1 uses a context-free grammar to describe the syntax of the mini-language. In particular, the following notations are used:

Figure 2.1 Mini-language Type.

```
program                 ::= program
                              variable-declaration...
                            begin
                              statement...
                            end ;
variable-declaration    ::= identifier [ , identifier ]... : type ;
type                    ::= simple-type | array-type | record-type
simple-type             ::= integer | boolean | string
array-type              ::= array [ bounds ] of type
record-type             ::= record
                              identifier : type ;
                              [ identifier : type ; ]...
                            end ;
bounds                  ::= integer .. integer
statement               ::= assignment-statement | if-statement
                          |   loop-statement | input-statement
                          |   output-statement
assignment-statement    ::= variable := expression ;
if-statement            ::= if ( expression )
                              if-option
                          [   else
                              if-option ]
if-option               ::= statement | { statement... }
loop-statement          ::= while expression loop
                              statement...
                            end loop ;
input-statement         ::= input   variable [ , variable ]... ;
output-statement        ::= output expression [ , expression ]... ;
expression              ::= operand [ operator operand ]
operand                 ::= integer | boolean | string | variable
                          | ( expression )
variable                ::= identifier | variable . identifier
                          |   variable [ expression ]
operator                ::= < | = | ≠ | > | + | - | * | div
                          |   and | or | cat
integer                 ::= digit...
string                  ::= " character... "
identifier              ::= letter [ letter | digit | _ ]...
boolean                 ::= true | false
character               ::= letter | digit | special-character
special-character       ::= b | + | - | * | / | : | ; | _
                          |   . | , | $ | % | < | = | ≠ | >
```

(a) *Productions*. The symbol ::= represents the name of a category (the left side) from its definition (the right side).

For instance, the production

    assignment-statement   ::=   variable := expression ;

is read

An assignment statement consists of a variable followed by a ":=" followed by an expression and a ";".

(b) *Alternatives*. The symbol "I" separates alternative forms of a construct.

For instance,

    operand   ::=   integer | boolean | string | variable

is read

An operand is either a variable, an integer, a boolean, a string, or a variable.

(c) *Optional Items*. Optional items are enclosed in square brackets.

For example,

    expression ::=   operand [operator operand]

is read

An expression consists of an operand optionally followed by an operator and a second operand.

When a square bracket stands for itself as a symbol in the language, the bracket is underlined. For instance, in

    array-type   ::=   array [bounds] of type

the brackets are part of the declaration of an array type.

(d) *Sequences*. Three dots (...) are used to indicate that an item or a bracketed item can be repeated an arbitrary number of times.

For example, the productions

```
integer           ::=      digit...
input-statement   ::=      input  variable [ , variable ]... ;
```

are read

An integer is a sequence of digits.

An input statement consists of the word "input" followed by a variable and, optionally, a sequence of other variables, each preceded by a comma.

A program in Mini-language Type consists of a sequence of declarations followed by a sequence of statements. The declarations specify the type of value that can be associated with each identifier. The statements define various actions.

Simple and Composite Types

A declaration specifies that a given list of identifiers can refer only to objects of the given type. The types in Mini-language Type are either simple or composite. The simple types include the integers (for example, 10 and 1776), strings of characters (for example, "ABC" and "123"), and the boolean values true and false. Note that the integer 123, denoting the numeric value one hundred and twenty-three, is different from the string "123", denoting the three characters for the digits representing one, two, and three.

The composite types in Mini-language Type are arrays of a given simple type and record structures. For example, an array TABLE with 10 integers is declared as

```
TABLE: array [1..10] of integer;
```

and a record structure VALUE representing a complex number is declared as

```
VALUE:
   record
      REAL: integer;
      IMAG: integer;
   end;
```

All identifiers referenced in the program must be declared exactly once.

A variable is either:

- An identifier.

- An identifier (or variable) denoting an array followed by a bracketed expression. The expression must be of type integer. In this case, the entire variable denotes some array component. This is a *subscripted reference*.

- An identifier (or variable) denoting a record followed by a dot and an identifier. The identifier after the dot must be the name of some component of the record associated with the first identifier (or variable). This is a *qualified reference*.

A reference to a variable must always have sufficient subscripts and qualifications so that the reference is to a simple integer, string, or boolean value. For example, using the earlier declaration of TABLE, the variable TABLE[3] is of type integer and denotes the third element of the array TABLE. Similarly, using the earlier declaration of COMPLEX_NUM, VALUE.REAL is of type integer and denotes a component of the record structure named VALUE.

Notice that if TABLE were declared to be an array of strings, then TABLE[3] would be of type string and the statement

```
TABLE[3] := 'XXXX';
```

would assign the string xxxx to the third element of TABLE.

Statements

There are five varieties of statements in Mini-language Type:

1. An assignment statement, which assigns the value of an expression to a variable. Both the variable and the expression must be of the same simple type.

2. An if statement, which executes a statement if the value of a conditional expression is true. The if statement may have an else part, which gives a statement to be executed if the value of the conditional expression is false. The conditional expression must be of boolean type.

3. A loop statement, which repeatedly executes a statement sequence as long as a conditional expression at the head of the loop is true.

4. An input statement, which reads in the values of one or more variables.

5. An output statement, which prints the values of one or more expressions.

For an input or output statement, each value must have a simple type.

Expressions

Variables may be combined by operators in an expression to form new values. The operators +, -, *, and div are defined over integers to yield their conventional results. The relational operators < and > are defined over integers and give a result of type boolean. The equality operators = and ≠ are defined over any two objects of the same simple type and also yield a result of type boolean.

The operators and and or are defined over two boolean values and perform the boolean "and" and "or" operations on the two values. The operator cat is defined over two string values and yields the string consisting of the concatenation of the two values.

For example, consider the declarations

```
X, Y, I, J: integer;
ITEM_FOUND, NO_MORE_ITEMS: boolean;
TEXT:  string;
TABLE: array[1..10] of integer;
ITEM:  array[1..10] of string;
VALUE: record
           REAL: integer;
           IMAG: integer;
       end;
```

The following expressions are legal:

Expressions of type integer:
```
223
(X + 2)
(X div 10)
(2 * (X - Y))
TABLE[I]
VALUE.REAL
```

Expressions of type string:
```
"UUW"
```

```
TEXT cat "ABC"
ITEM[I] cat ("A" cat ITEM[J])
```

Expressions of type boolean:
```
true
(ITEM[I] = "A")
TABLE[I] = VALUE.REAL
ITEM_FOUND
ITEM_FOUND or NO_MORE_ITEMS
```

Here we see a number of expressions whose values are integer, string, or boolean.

Note: For simplicity, no precedence rules specifying the order of operations are given for Mini-language Type, as all expressions with more than one operator must be parenthesized.

Examples

The following program is illegal:

```
program
    A: integer;
begin
    A := "XYZ"; -- A is not of type string
end;
```

This example shows a fundamental property of most languages with several types. Once a variable is declared to have a certain type, in this case, integer, the type cannot be changed during execution. It is thus illegal to assign values of another type (for example, string) to it.

The next program is also illegal:

```
program
    A, B: integer;
begin
    A := 0;
    B := (3 or A); -- "or" is an illegal operation for
integers
end;
```

The error here is in the attempt to use an operation that is only applicable to boolean values and applying it to two integer values.

The next example can give an error during execution:

PROBLEM

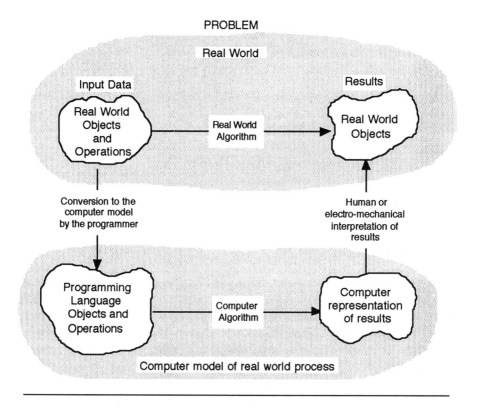

Figure 2.2 Model of a typical programming task.

```
program
    A: integer;
begin
    input A;    -- input value might not be an integer
    A := A + 1;
    output A;
end;
```

If a variable is declared to be of a certain type and thus can take on only values within that type, an attempt to input a value of a different type will result in an error during execution. In particular, if the input statement attempts to read a string or a boolean value, an execution error occurs.

Finally, the following shows a program that adds two complex numbers:

```
program
    I, J, RESULT:
```

```
        record
            REAL: integer;
            IMAG: integer;
        end;
    begin
        input I.REAL, I.IMAG;
        input J.REAL, J.IMAG;
        RESULT.REAL := I.REAL + J.REAL;
        RESULT.IMAG := I.IMAG + J.IMAG;
        output RESULT.REAL, RESULT.IMAG;
    end;
```

This illustrates the use of record variables.

2.2   THE MEANING OF TYPE

A view of programming is shown in Figure 2.2. The problem to be solved by the computer is presented as a real-world algorithm that manipulates real-world objects. For example, the algorithm may take objects such as names, hours worked, and salaries and produce a payroll. To model the algorithm, the programmer must choose a representation of the objects in the problem from the possibilities afforded by the programming language.

The choice of representation can have a great effect on the clarity and correctness of the computer algorithm. Thus, for example, a floating-point number would not be a suitable representation of a telephone number because there are likely to be inaccuracies introduced in converting it to and from the real-world form. The number is used only for identification, so we never perform arithmetic operations on it. It would make no sense to talk about the average telephone number of one's friends. A character-string representation would be better in this case.

With each set of objects of a particular type that can be manipulated in a programming language, there is a corresponding set of operations that can be performed on objects. In Mini-language Type, addition, subtraction, multiplication, division, and the four comparison operations can be performed on integer objects. Concatenation and tests of equality and inequality are the valid operations for string objects.

A consequence of a particular choice of representation of a real-world object is the set of operations that can be performed on the object in the model. Each operation used in a program should have a corresponding meaning in the real world. For example, suppose dates were represented by integers. Although two dates may be subtracted to give a time interval, there is no analog of the addition, multiplication, or division of dates in the real world. Thus,

```
DATE1, DATE2: integer;
...
DATE1 := DATE1 + DATE2;
```

is meaningless.

This view of programming leads to a definition of types:

A type is a collection of objects and a set of operations that can be validly performed on the objects.

For instance, the type dollars may be viewed as a collection of quantities, $1, $2, etc., along with certain operations. For example, it is meaningful to "add" or "subtract" two dollar amounts to yield another dollar amount. It is also meaningful to "multiply" a dollar amount by an integer or a percentage to yield another dollar amount.

Generally, types such as dates, dollars, and percentages are not included directly within a programming language. Rather, most programming languages, like Mini-language Type, provide a few basic types that the programmer must use to define meaningful computations on a class of real-world objects.

2.3 PRIMITIVE TYPES

In this section, we discuss several kinds of primitive types: boolean types, integer types, and other numeric types.

Boolean Types

Perhaps the simplest of all types found in programming is the boolean type. This type contains only two values, true and false. Operations on values of this type vary from language to language, as do the operations for almost every type. Typical operators include

not	a unary operator for negating a boolean value
or	a binary operator for the logical "or" of two boolean values
and	a binary operator for the logical "and" of two boolean values

Thus, we may view the "type" boolean as

{false, true}	the collection of objects	
not	boolean => boolean	a unary operation
or	boolean, boolean) => boolean	a binary operation
and	(boolean, boolean) => boolean	a binary operation
input	an operation that reads a boolean value	
output	an operation that prints a boolean value	

In general, the evaluation of an expression of the form

operand operator operand

involves the evaluation of both operands before the complete expression can be evaluated. The properties of the *and* and *or* operators make it sometimes possible to evaluate the complete expression without evaluating the second operand. For the *or* operation, if the value of the first operand is true, then the value of the complete expression will be true, regardless of the value of the second operand. Similarly, for the *and* operation, if the value of the first operand is false, then, whatever the value of the second operand, the value of the complete expression will be false.

Some languages do not have boolean values in the pure sense. For example, in C, the value 0 is treated as false and any non-zero value is treated as true. Cobol allows only indirect use of boolean values. It permits conditional expressions; for example,

```
IF (X = Y) ...
```

but does not permit boolean-valued variables or functions that return boolean values.

Character and String Types

The manipulation of characters is fundamental to many programming problems because communication with users is generally via sequences of characters. The real requirement is not to handle characters by themselves, but to manipulate sequences of several characters. These sequences are usually known as *strings*.

There are two kinds of operations that can be performed on strings:

1. Those that treat strings in their entirety: comparison, assignment, and building longer strings through concatenation.

2. Those that require the decomposition of strings into substrings.

Some languages provide a special primitive type for a string. Other languages treat strings as a sequence of characters or as an array of characters.

Numeric Types

Numerical calculations have always had an important role in the use of computers. All programming languages manipulate numeric data. Even in languages designed for nonnumeric work, Snobol for example, there is a need for numbers to act as counters, field widths, and control values in computation.

Numeric types generally fall into one of three classes:

1. *Integer:* used for exact arithmetic on whole numbers within a fixed range.

2. *Fixed point:* used for noninteger values with a fixed number of digits before and after the radix point.

3. *Floating point:* used for noninteger values with a fixed number of significant digits and a widely varying magnitude.

We can picture the type integer as

```
{... -2, -1, 0, 1, 2, ...}      the collection of objects

+(integer, integer) => integer  the addition of two values
-(integer, integer) => integer  the subtraction of two values
*(integer, integer) => integer  the multiplication of two values
÷(integer, integer) => integer  the division of two values
```

$<, >, =, \neq$ (integer, integer) => boolean operations from two integers into a boolean value

input   an operation that reads an integer value
output   an operation that prints an integer value

The written form of numeric values is largely determined by

conventional usage. To aid readability, some languages allow a break character to divide lengthy sequences of digits. For example, the denotations

```
1000000    -- C, Mini-language Type
1 000 000  -- Algol 60, Fortran
1_000_000  -- Ada, Eiffel
```

are different ways of writing the same integer.

An important difference between the numeric values in programming languages and those in mathematics is that the computer values all have finite representations. Thus, they are frequently approximations to their real-world equivalents. There is no way that a completely accurate value of pi can be represented in a computer. The need to represent objects with a wide range of numeric values, even if the representations are approximate, gives rise to fixed point and the floating point form.

The written representation of fixed point numbers is generally of the form:

digit-sequence . digit-sequence

For clarity, neither digit sequence should be null and the radix point should always be required. Floating point numbers can represent objects with a wide range of values. The written form of floating point values has an essential difference from integer and fixed point values because of the need for an exponent. The beginning of the exponent part is usually marked with the letter E, for example:

```
3.14259E0
10E+2
```

With the preceding syntax rules, it is possible to determine the type of all written numeric values. In languages where there are no implicit type conversions, it is possible to enforce the rule that only constants of the appropriate type can be used in assignments and expressions. This discipline has the important advantage that different types of arithmetic are distinguished; the exact computations are separated from the approximate.

Overloading

One feature that is common to the three numeric types is the set of arithmetic operators. Although these operators are written with the same symbol for each type, they specify somewhat different actions. For example,

+ can denote integer addition, fixed point addition, or floating point addition. Integer addition has no radix point. Fixed point addition maintains the position of the radix point, whereas floating point addition adjusts position of the radix point to accommodate a range of values.

The use of a single symbol to denote an operation whose meaning is determined by the operand types is called *overloading*. Probably the two most common overloaded operations are the relations = and ≠, which generally apply to all types.

As well as denoting addition of arithmetic operands, the symbol + is sometimes used to denote concatenation of string operands. The + operator is then an overloaded operator, the meaning of which changes considerably as its operand types change.

Type Conversions

In our everyday pencil-and-paper calculations, we treat all numeric data as being of a single type, numbers. We do not think whether they are integers, rationals, or irrationals. In programming, things are not so simple; there are different numeric types with separate representations.

In Mini-language Type, there is only one numeric type, integer, so the problem of assigning one type of numeric value to a variable of another does not arise. In most languages, this problem exists and these assignments are usually allowed. The same numeric value may have different representations in separate numeric types. The mappings between these representations are generally called *type conversions*.

When the type conversion is implicit, the term *coercion* is sometimes used. Conversions from integer to fixed point, from fixed point to floating point, and from floating point to complex can generally be done without loss of information. A conversion of this sort is called a widening.

As the number of numeric data types in a language increases, so does the number of possible conversions. Some languages, for example, Pascal and Ada, insist that almost all conversions be done through the explicit use of a function. For example, to convert a real value V to an integer in Ada, the function call INTEGER(V) is used. At the other end of the scale, C has the deliberate policy of defining the mappings between data types whenever they have a reasonable meaning. These implicit conversions can lead to programming errors that are accepted by the compiler as a reasonable conversion. The advantage of the Pascal and Ada kind of approach is that the programmer is made aware of almost all conversions.

2.4 COMPOSITE TYPES

The modeling of objects, such as a deck of cards, a birth certificate, or a bank account, brings up the general issue of *composite* types. Objects of a composite type are not indivisible, but have components bearing some relation to each other. Every programming language offers one or more built-in composite types. Among others, Fortran has arrays, Cobol has record structures, Pascal has sets, Lisp has lists, and APL has vectors.

The composite types in a language affect the ease with which real-world objects can be represented. For example, representing a bank account is quite easy in Cobol, and representing a network is quite easy in Lisp, but not necessarily vice versa.

Array Types

The array is perhaps the most familiar composite type in programming. An array is basically a mapping from a range of contiguous integers to a set of elements. These integer values are called the *index* or *subscript* values. Usually, languages permit arrays to have more than one index.

In its simplest form, an array is a representation of a table. For example, consider a table that represents the number of people waiting in line at each of five counters. In Mini-language Type, this array might be declared by

```
QUEUE: array [1..5] of integer;
```

An important property of an array is that the value of any one of its elements can be changed without affecting the value of any of the other elements. An element of an array, for example, A[3], behaves like a variable of the element type.

The range of index values of an array defines the number of elements of the array; this is the *size* of the array. In most programming languages, the range of index values must be specified by the programmer.

The point at which the size of an array must be known is a subject of considerable difference in programming languages. For example, consider the following cases:

```
A: array [1..5] of integer;
```

Here the size of the array is defined at the time the declaration is written:

```
N: integer constant = 5;
A: array [1..N] of integer;
```

Here the size of the array is defined at the time the declaration of the constant N and the array declaration are written.

Next, consider

```
procedure F (N: integer) is
    A: array [1..N] of integer;
    ...
end;
```

In this procedure fragment, N is a parameter whose value is established when the procedure is invoked. Thus, the size of the array is only determined at execution time and can vary from one invocation to another. Such an array is called a *dynamic array.*

Record Types

A programmer must often deal with objects having a number of different components. For example, a driving license may be viewed as an object having the following:

Driver:	a name consisting of a
First name:	a string of letters
Middle initial:	a single letter
Last name:	a string of letters
License number:	eight digits
Expiration date:	a calendar date consisting of a
Month:	a number from 1 to 12
Day:	a number from 1 to 31
Year:	a four digit number
Driving code:	a character

The type used for collections of related objects is often called a *record.* Basically, a record type contains a collection of components, each of which may be of a different type. Each component has a name and a value.

For example, a record of type LICENSE can be declared in Mini-language Type by

```
LICENSE: record
    DRIVER: record
            FIRST_NAME:      string;
            MIDDLE_INITIAL: string;
            LAST_NAME:       string;
        end;
```

```
LICENSE_NUM: string;
EXPIRATION:  record
          MONTH: integer;
          DAY:   integer;
          YEAR:  integer;
       end;
    DRIVING_CODE: string;
end;
```

Notice, for example, that though the original description of the license specifies the license number as a number, it is really a sequence of digits. It does not make sense to multiply a license number by 5. Similarly, the month, day, and year of expiration are not really integers, although it is convenient to perform limited numerical calculations, for example, computing when to send out the renewal notice two months before expiration.

The basic operation on record types is component selection. For example, to refer to the driving code component, we write

```
LICENSE.DRIVING_CODE
```

This is the method used in Ada, Pascal, C, and Euclid. Algol 68 and Cobol take a different point of view, by writing

```
DRIVING CODE of LICENSE -- Algol 68
DRIVING-CODE in LICENSE -- Cobol
```

This approach seems to focus more attention on the component, whereas the Ada, Pascal, C, and Euclid view attaches more importance to the record as a whole.

The value of the reference LICENSE.DRIVER is also a record, so that it is possible to write

```
LICENSE.DRIVER.LAST_NAME
```

A reference to a record component behaves just as a reference to the component of an array. For example, we may have

```
LICENSE.LICENSE_NUM := '022325795';
LICENSE.EXPIRATION.YEAR := LICENSE.EXPIRATION.YEAR + 4;
```

The basic difference between the method of selecting components in arrays and records is that in arrays, the component can be calculated by means of a subscript expression evaluated at the time of reference. With a record, the component must be selected at the time the program is written; the choice cannot be changed during execution.

Variant Records

In the license example, the driving code may indicate a special or a restricted permit; such a permit may require other information. This kind of structure is generally handled with a record *variant*.

A record type with a variant part must have a special component called a *tag* and a selection mechanism giving the various substructures for possible values of the tag. For the selection mechanism denoting the variant, we shall use a caselike notation, similar to that for case statements. This method is borrowed from Ada.

To represent our license example in full, we can write the declaration of Example 2.1. Here, the component DRIVING_CODE is used as a tag, and the following case structure defines the record variant. When the value of the tag is S, the information for a special vehicle type is included; when its value is R, the information for a restricted permit is included.

Selecting a component of a variant record is just the same as for an ordinary record. Thus, provided that the value of the tag field DRIVING_CODE is 'S', we may reference LICENSE.PASSENGER_PERMIT. However, it would be an error to reference LICENSE.DAYLIGHT_ONLY. This field does not exist when the value of the tag field is 'S'. It only exists when the tag's value is 'R'. If an assignment is made to the tag field to change its value, the components of the old variant are destroyed and the components of the new variant are created.

Each variant of a record type can take a separate set of values. Thus, the complete record type with all its variants can take the union of these sets of values. It is common to refer to such record types as *unions* and to refer to those that contain a tag field to distinguish between the variants as *discriminated unions*. Those unions where the language does not insist on the tag field are known as *free unions*.

Variant records implicitly bring up a topic in object-oriented programming. This topic is *subtypes*. In the previous case, special and restricted licenses are natural situations for defining derived types. A restricted license, for instance, can be considered a new type that inherits the properties (e.g., the fields) of the type LICENSE. Subtypes and inheritance are major topics discussed later in this work.

2.5   TYPE CHECKING

The partitioning of objects into types allows each assignment to be checked for a match between source value and target variable. The validity of each

```
LICENSE: record
   DRIVER: record
                 FIRST_NAME:      string;
                 LAST_NAME:       string;
                 MIDDLE_INITIAL: string;
            end;
   LICENSE_NUM: string;
   DRIVING_CODE: string; -- tag
   case DRIVING_CODE of
      when 'S' =>
         VEHICLE_TYPE:      integer;
         PASSENGER_PERMIT: boolean;
         ZONE_CODE:          boolean;
      when 'R' =>
         CORRECTIVE_LENSES: boolean;
         DAYLIGHT_ONLY:      boolean;
         AUTO_TRANSMISSION: boolean;
      else => null;
   end case;
   EXPIRATION_DATE:
      record
         MONTH: integer;
         DAY:    integer;
         YEAR:   integer;
      end;
end;
```

Example 2.1   A record variant.

operation for its operands can also be verified. If these tests can be made during compilation, *before* execution, then we say that the type checking is *static*. Ada and Fortran, for example, have static type checking. These two languages allow the type checking to be complete, although the type checking may not be done rigorously in all implementations. Such languages are said to be *strongly typed*. Pascal, because it allows the tag field of variant records to be changed, has exceptions to strong typing.

If the type checking can only be done *during* execution, then the type checking is *dynamic*. Smalltalk is a dynamically typed language.

The essential difference between statically and dynamically typed languages is that in a statically typed language, the type is associated with an identifier. In a dynamically typed language, the type is associated with the value. This is implemented by storing type information with each value. Any type of value can be assigned to a variable. Before any operation is applied to a value, the type of the value is examined to see if it is compatible with the operation. In the case of overloaded operations, the type of the value will determine the precise details of how the operation is to be performed.

Because dynamic type checking is performed during execution, there is a machine time penalty. Furthermore, because type errors can only be found by execution, it is generally impossible to verify that a program contains no type errors. It is often claimed that dynamic typing allows the programmer greater flexibility; however, it is not clear that this gain is sufficient to offset the loss of reliability.

Object-oriented languages introduce a subtlety of typechecking due to inheritance, classes, and subclasses. One type (or class) can be a subtype (or subclass) of another. A variable of a given class can be assigned values of different subclasses of the class. Hence an operation applied to a value may only apply to a selected subclass, and a check for compatibility must wait until run-time.

Some languages avoid the idea of type altogether. These are generally the high-level *systems programming* languages. Examples of such languages are Bliss and BCPL. In Bliss, any contiguous set of bits in storage can be named, and from the language's point of view, merely contains a pattern of bits. Various operations, such as integer arithmetic, comparison, or boolean operations, may be applied to these bit patterns. The interpretation placed on a particular bit pattern and the consequent transformation performed by the operator is an intrinsic property of the operator and not of its operands.

The argument for type checking is one of security. The rationale behind static type checking, as opposed to dynamic type checking, is that a number of errors can be detected before the program is allowed to run. The counterargument is that strong typing removes some of the flexibility that programmers find useful, particularly in systems programming.

FURTHER READING

In the literature, works solely on the concept of type have been overshadowed by the rather large effort in the areas discussed later in this work. Nevertheless, we mention a few relevant references.

An early work [Morris 1973] discusses the now prevalent view of a type, which is characterized by a set of objects as well as operations over the objects. A later paper [Brosgol 1977] discusses a number of issues relevant to types. Type issues are also extensively discussed in the rationale for the preliminary version of Ada [Ichbiah et al. 1979].

A comprehensive discussion of the entire type area is given in the book An Introduction to Data Types by J. Craig Cleaveland [Cleaveland 1986].

EXERCISES

Exercise 2.1 *Multiple Choice*

Pick the answer that best fits the question.

1. A primary goal of OOP is
   a. to prove programs correct.
   b. improved software reliability.
   c. greater productivity.
   d. to be able to work in teams
   e. a reduction of global variables.

2. Which of the following is not a keyword in Mini-language Type?
   a. `loop`
   b. `program`
   c. `array`
   d. `output`
   e. `do`

3. In Mini-language Type,
   a. the type of every expression is known at compile time.
   b. explicit conversions between string values and integer values are not allowed.
   c. the expression at the head of a while loop must be boolean.
   d. arrays of records are allowed.
   e. all of the above.

4. A record variant is
   a. a field of a record that can have various types.
   b. an assertion that can vary according to the fields of a record.
   c. a record with pointer fields.
   d. a record with varying substructures.
   e. all of the above.

5. Which of the following is least likely to be represented as an array?
   a. A set of passwords.
   b. A chessboard.

   c.   A telephone bill.
   d.   A directory.
   e.   A string of characters.
6. A coercion is
   a.   an implied type conversion.
   b.   an overloaded operation.
   c.   a construct in Pascal.
   d.   an implicit record variant.
   e.   a binary representation.
7. Which of the following data types would most closely represent a telephone number?
   a.   An integer.
   b.   A string.
   c.   A floating point number.
   d.   A record.
   e.   A record variant.

Exercise 2.2 *Programming in Mini-language Type*

On many computer systems, a calendar date is expressed in six-digit form. For example,

    02 22 43

means the month 02, day 22, year 1943, or in more familiar terms, we use day-to-day NOTATION:

    FEBRUARY 22, 1943

Write a program in Mini-language Type to read in three integer numbers and output the corresponding date in day-to-day notation. If the integers do not represent a valid date, an appropriate message should be printed. For example, with

    13 22 43

the output should be

    NOT A VALID DATE

Don't forget about leap year.

Exercise 2.3 *Mixed Mode*

Some languages with multiple data types (modes) allow mixed mode expressions, where an expression may involve operands of different types; the operands are converted at run time if necessary to compatible modes before the operators are applied. In other languages, operands that are not of the correct mode for an operation must be explicitly converted by using a set of functions provided in the language for that purpose.

For example, if J were an integer, in C, one could write the expression

```
(J + '3')
```

whereas in the other class of languages, one would have to write this as

```
(J + CHAR_TO_INT('3'))
```

where CHAR_TO_INT is a function that performs character string to integer conversion. What are the advantages and disadvantages of each scheme?

Exercise 2.4 *Literals for Arrays*

In some languages, it is possible to write values for both composite objects and for simple objects. For example, in Ada, a 10 element array A may be set to zero with the assignment:

```
A := (1..10 => 0); -- named notation
```

For a five-element array where elements are 11, 14, 10, 16, and 11, we may write

```
(11, 14, 10, 16, 11) -- positional notation
```

where the array elements are listed in positioned order, or alternatively,

```
(1 => 11; 2 => 14; 3 => 10; 4 => 16; 5 => 11) -- named
                                              -- notation
```

where the index values are identified. Discuss the pros and cons of these two notations.

Exercise 2.5 *Array Access*

Consider a language in which arrays may have many dimensions. The number of dimensions and the bounds on the dimensions are fixed by the declaration and may not be changed dynamically. Suppose a particular array has n dimensions with lower bounds l_1, l_2, through l_n and upper bounds u_1, u_2, through u_n and that the array is stored as a contiguous set of elements. Describe how the location of a particular element of the array can be calculated from its subscripts.

Exercise 2.6 *Array Operations*

Consider an extension to Mini-language Type so that arrays are treated as complete objects. That is to say, they may be used in assignments and as operands of operations. Define the changes to the syntax and semantics of this extended version of Type.

Exercise 2.7 *The Mod Operator*

Find out how the mod operator is defined for negative operands in three different languages and discuss their usefulness to the programmer.

CHAPTER 3

Definition of New Types

Types allow the programmer to organize and express a solution to a problem by naming and identifying specific ideas about data.

. . .

Typing helps us see the properties of what we are dealing with.

. . .

A type system allows us to restrict attention to a particular kind of object.

[J. Craig Cleaveland 1986]

Types allow the programmer to organize and express a solution to a problem by naming and identifying specific ideas about data. Different areas of application, for example, data processing, graphics, operations research, or text preparation, require different abstractions with specialized properties. With object-oriented programming, we want to represent the objects and operations of an application properly. This means defining new data types. Facilities for defining new data types were not directly available in early languages like Fortran and Basic. With these languages, the programmer must make mental associations between the objects and operations in the real world of the application and the structured data objects that represent them in the program.

Languages such as Pascal, Simula 67, Modula-2, Clu, Ada, C++, and Eiffel have various facilities for defining types. To varying extents, these languages enable the application programmer to define particular objects and operations, that is, to define new data types. The application program can then be written using newly defined types and their operations. In essence, the programmer can create a dialect of the original language that more closely matches the application.

In this chapter, the beginnings of a user-defined type mechanism is explored using Mini-language Typedef. This mechanism goes beyond that provided in Pascal because it provides for the definition of operators as well as for classes of values. Mini-language Typedef is a major step toward object-oriented programming.

Most importantly, the spirit of object-oriented programming is captured by the elementary methods discussed in this chapter. Put another way, the approach to programming in this chapter is, in a broad sense, object-oriented.

3.1   MINI-LANGUAGE TYPEDEF

The syntax of Mini-language Typedef is given in Figure 3.1. Mini-language Typedef has many features similar to the Mini-language Type given earlier. A program in Mini-language Typedef consists of a declarative part followed by a sequence of statements

There are three kinds of declarations: type declarations, operator declarations, and variable declarations. A variable declaration associates one or more identifiers with the type integer or with a type that has been defined in a type declaration. Integers have the usual meaning and operations. All identifiers in a program must be declared exactly once.

Declaration of New Types

The major item of interest in Mini-language Typedef lies in the declaration of new types and operations. For example, we may have

```
type DAY_NAME  = (MON, TUE, WED, THU, FRI, SAT, SUN);
type SUIT_NAME = (CLUBS, DIAMONDS, HEARTS, SPADES);
```

The first declaration introduces a type named DAY_NAME. Just as we can say

```
COUNTER: integer;
```

Figure 3.1 Mini-language Typedef.

```
program                ::= program
                           [ type-declaration... ]
                           [ operator-declaration... ]
                             variable-declaration...
                           begin
                             statement...
                           end ;
type-declaration       ::= type identifier =  type-definition ;
                        |  subtype identifier = subtype-definition ;
operator-declaration   ::= operator operator operator-type
                           [ variable-declaration ]...
                           begin
                             statement...
                             return expression ;
                           end ;
operator-type          ::= ( identifier : type-name , identifier :
                             type-name ) => type-name
variable-declaration   ::= identifier [ , identifier ]... : type-name ;
type-name              ::= integer | boolean | string | identifier
type-definition        ::= enumerated-type | array-type
enumerated-type        ::= ( identifier [ , identifier ]... )
subtype-definition     ::= type-name range
range                  ::= value .. value
value                  ::= integer | identifier
array-type             ::= array [ range ] of type-name
statement              ::= assignment-statement | if-statement
                        |  loop-statement | input-statement | output-statement
assignment-            ::= variable := expression ;
statement
if-statement           ::= if ( expression )
                             if-option
                        [  else
                             if-option ]
if-option              ::= statement | { statement... }
loop-statement         ::= while expression loop
                             statement...
                           end loop ;
                        |  for identifier := range loop
                             statement...
                           end loop ;
```

Figure 3.1   (continued)

input-statement	::=	input variable [, variable]... ;
output-statement	::=	output expression [, expression]... ;
expression	::=	operand [operator operand]
operand	::=	integer | boolean | string | variable
		| (expression)
variable	::=	identifier
		| variable ⌞ expression ⌟
operator	::=	< | = | ≠ | > | + | − | * | div
		| and | or

to declare a variable COUNTER of type integer, we can say

```
TODAY  : DAY_NAME;
TRUMPS: SUIT_NAME;
```

to declare a variable TODAY of type DAY_NAME and a variable TRUMPS of type SUIT_NAME.

Just as a variable of type integer can only take integer values, a variable of type DAY_NAME can only take one of the seven values MON through SUN. The two types just introduced are called *enumerated types* because the type declarations explicitly enumerate the class of values.

For simplicity, an identifier can only appear in one enumerated type. Thus, the pair of declarations

```
type TRAFFIC_LIGHT = (RED, AMBER, GREEN);
type FLAG_COLOR    = (RED, WHITE, BLUE);
```

is not allowed.

Variables declared with the new types behave much like variables declared of type integer. They can be assigned to variables of the same type and have values assigned to them from constants belonging to that class of values.

For example, we may have

```
TODAY    := MON;
NEW_COIN := NICKEL;
```

but not

```
SUN   := MON;     -- only variables can be assigned values
TODAY := 1;       -- types do not match
TODAY := NICKEL; -- types do not match
```

The input and output facilities of Mini-language Typedef also apply to values of enumerated types. When applied to an enumerated variable, an input statement gets the next item in the input stream, checks that it is the character representation for a value of the enumerated type of the variable, and sets this value to the corresponding variable. Similarly, an output statement prints the character representation corresponding to the enumerated value of the variable.

Subtypes

Restricted sequences or subranges of both integer and enumerated types can be defined by a *subtype*. The purpose of a subtype is to limit the set of values that a variable may take during execution. For example, we may have

```
subtype YEAR_NUM   = integer  1776..2001;
subtype COLUMN_POS = integer  1..72;
subtype WEEKDAY    = DAY_NAME MON..FRI;
subtype WEEKEND    = DAY_NAME SAT..SUN;
```

A subtype is thus characterized by two properties:

- *The parent type:* For instance, the parent type of YEAR_NUM is integer; the parent type of WEEKDAY is DAY_NAME.

- *The bounds of the range:* For instance, 1776 and 2001 are the bounds for the type YEAR_NUM. The bounds specify the first and last values of the subtype. The bounds also determine the *range size*, which is the number of elements in the range. For instance, the range size of WEEKDAY is 5.

Both the first and last bounds of a range must be of the same type as the parent type. For integer subtypes, the bounds must be stated in increasing order. For subtypes of enumerated types, the bounds must be stated in the same order as they are declared. For example, the following subtype definitions are illegal:

```
SUIT_NAME range 1..HEARTS; -- bounds not of the same type
DAY_NAME  range FRI..TUE;  -- bounds not in order
integer   range 17..12;    -- bounds not in order
```

Variables of a subtype are declared just as variables of other types. Examples are

```
WORK_DAY:  WEEKDAY;
THIS_YEAR: YEAR_NUM;
```

The type of such variables is the same as the parent type.

Array Types

The types definable in Mini-language Typedef include array types. For example, we may declare the array types

```
type INPUT_LINE  = array [1..72]    of integer;
type WEEK_VALUE  = array [MON..FRI] of integer;
type CALENDAR    = array [1..31]    of DAY_NAME;
```

and the array variables

```
INPUT_VALUE : INPUT_LINE;
HOURS_WORKED: WEEK_VALUE;
JANUARY     : CALENDAR;
```

As for subtypes, the bounds of an array type must belong to a declared enumerated type or to the predefined type integer.

The individual components of an array can be referenced, for example,

```
INPUT_VALUE[2]     -- the second input value
INPUT_VALUE[I]     -- the Ith input value
HOURS_WORKED[WED] -- the number of hours worked on
                   -- Wednesday
```

Any attempt to use a subscript outside the bounds declared for the array variable results in an execution error.

Statements

The statements in Mini-language Typedef are conventional. In an assignment statement, the variable and the expression must have the same type. There are two kinds of loop statements in Mini-language Typedef: the while loop and the for loop. In a while loop, the sequence of statements in the body of the loop is executed repeatedly as long as the condition at the head of the loop remains true. In a for loop, the head of the loop defines a range of values that is to be assigned to a control variable. The sequence of statements that form the body of the loop is executed for each value in the range. Thus, in the loop

```
for DAY := MON..FRI loop
    TOTAL_HOURS := TOTAL_HOURS + HOURS_WORKED[DAY];
end loop;
```

the body of the loop will be executed five times with the control variable DAY successively taking the values MON through FRI. A control-loop variable cannot be assigned a new value within the loop.

Expressions

The operators = and ≠ are defined for all types and can be used to compare the values of variables for equality with others of the same type. Thus, if TODAY has the value MON, we may have the following comparisons:

```
(TODAY = TUE) -- comparison is false
(TODAY = MON) -- comparison is true
```

The operators = and ≠ are the only overloaded operators in the mini-language; all the rest of the operators are only defined for integers. The operators +, minus, and * are conventional arithmetic operators, and the div operator provides integer division.

The operations of a subtype are those that are applicable to the parent type. For subtypes whose parent type is integer, the arithmetic operators apply as well.

Expressions including variables and constants of various types are allowed, provided that operations are applied only to values for which the operation is defined. For instance, consider the following:

```
(TODAY = MON) -- valid if TODAY is of type DAY_NAME
X + Y         -- valid if X and Y are of type integer
```

The context in which expressions may appear may require the result value to be restricted to a specified range. Any attempt to assign a value that lies outside of the declared range will result in an execution error. Examples of range variable assignments in Mini-language Typedef are

```
WORK_DAY  := TUE;              -- always valid
THIS_YEAR := THIS_YEAR + 50;  -- can lead to execution error
```

In general, exceeding a declared range can only be detected during execution. However, it is important to note that sensible use of ranges allows system detection of range errors. Without a range specification, there would be no hint of wrongdoing until some doubtful results appear in the program output.

Declaration of Operations

As emphasized in Chapter 2, a data type implies more than just a class of values. There is also a collection of operations that can be performed on the values. In Mini-language Typedef, the symbols <, =, ≠, >, +, −, *, div, cat, and, and or, denote operators. For these operators to be applied to other types of values, their meaning must be defined through operator declarations. These new operator definitions overload the operators with new meanings outside those predefined in Mini-language Typedef.

For example, given the type SUIT_NAME, we can define the comparison operator < as follows:

```
operator < (S1: SUIT_NAME, S2: SUIT_NAME) => boolean
   -- S1 is the left operand
   -- S2 is the right operand
   RESULT: boolean;
begin
   if (S1 = S2)
      RESULT := false;
   else
      if (S1 = CLUBS)
         RESULT := true;
      else
         if (S2 = CLUBS)
            RESULT := false;
         else
            if (S1 = DIAMONDS)
               RESULT := true;
            else
               if (S2 = DIAMONDS)
                  RESULT := false;
               else
                  if (S1 = HEARTS)
                     RESULT := true;
                  else
                     RESULT := false;
```

```
     return RESULT;
  end;
```

The heading of the operator definition,

```
operator < (S1: SUIT_NAME, S2: SUIT_NAME) =>  boolean
```

shows that there are two operands of type SUIT_NAME and the type of the value produced by the operation will be boolean. The value returned by the operation is specified in the return statement at the end of the operation specification. With the preceding definitions, we may write code such as

```
SUIT: SUIT_NAME:
...
if (SUIT < HEARTS) {
   ...
}
...
```

The types of the two operands for an operation do not need to be the same. Consider, for example, the following operator declaration for adding an elapsed number of days to a DAY_NAME value to obtain a new DAY_NAME value:

```
operator + (DAY: DAY_NAME, INT: integer) => DAY_NAME
   I, DAY_INDEX: integer;
   DAY_VALUE:   array[1..7] of DAY_NAME;
begin
   DAY_VALUE[1] := MON;
   DAY_VALUE[2] := TUE;
   DAY_VALUE[3] := WED;
   DAY_VALUE[4] := THU;
   DAY_VALUE[5] := FRI;
   DAY_VALUE[6] := SAT;
   DAY_VALUE[7] := SUN;
   for I := 1..7 loop
      if (DAY = DAY_VALUE[I])
         DAY_INDEX := I;
   end loop;
   DAY_INDEX := DAY_INDEX + INT;
   DAY_INDEX := DAY_INDEX - 7*((DAY_INDEX - 1) div 7) ;
               -- reduce DAY_INDEX modulo 7
   return DAY_VALUE[DAY_INDEX];
end;
```

An operator declaration can refer to previously defined operators. Thus, the converse version of the preceding operator, adding an integer to a DAY_NAME, can be defined as

```
operator + (DAY: integer, INT: DAY_NAME) => DAY_NAME
begin
    return DAY + INT;
end;
```

An Example

As a simple illustration of the power of user-defined types, we present Example 3.1. This example illustrates the basic idea that a program can introduce a type to describe a class of values needed for an application. The program reads in an initial compass direction followed by a sequence of course changes and computes a final course direction. The body of the program is very simple. The computation is expressed in terms of adding a change to a course to get a new course and is thus natural to the problem being solved. In addition, the input is expressed in natural values such as NORTH and REVERSE.

Solving the same problem in a language where it is not possible to define new types would be more difficult. Directions and headings would have to be encoded into integers and the logic would be more difficult to understand. Even if a look-up table were used, checking the correctness of the program would be more difficult than the one shown in Example 3.1

3.2   TYPE DEFINITIONS

In Mini-language Typedef, programmer-defined types are introduced by type declarations of the form

type identifier = type-definition ;

The identifier specifies a name for the type. The type definition specifies the class of values.

Except for subtypes of other defined types, every type definition introduces a distinct type. Separate declarations define operations that can manipulate the values of a type.

We recall the basic definition of a type given earlier:

```
program
    -- This program reads in a compass direction followed
    -- by a sequence of 20 course changes.
    -- The program prints the final course direction.

    type DIRECTION = (NORTH, EAST, SOUTH, WEST);
    type TURN      = (RIGHT, REVERSE, LEFT);
    COURSE: DIRECTION;
    CHANGE: TURN;
    COUNTER: integer;

    operator + (D: DIRECTION, ALTERATION: TURN) =>  DIRECTION
        type VECTOR = array [RIGHT..LEFT] of DIRECTION;
        TABLE: array [NORTH..WEST] of VECTOR;
    begin
        TABLE[NORTH, RIGHT]    := EAST;
        TABLE[NORTH, REVERSE]  := SOUTH;
        TABLE[NORTH, LEFT]     := WEST;
        TABLE[EAST,  RIGHT]    := SOUTH;
        TABLE[EAST,  REVERSE]  := WEST;
        TABLE[EAST,  LEFT]     := NORTH;
        TABLE[SOUTH, RIGHT]    := WEST;
        TABLE[SOUTH, REVERSE]  := NORTH;
        TABLE[SOUTH, LEFT]     := EAST;
        TABLE[WEST,  RIGHT]    := NORTH;
        TABLE[WEST,  REVERSE]  := EAST;
        TABLE[WEST,  LEFT]     := SOUTH;
        return TABLE[D, ALTERATION];
    end;

begin
    input COURSE;
    for COUNTER := 1..20 loop
        input CHANGE;
        COURSE := COURSE + CHANGE;
    end loop;
    output COURSE;
end;
```

Example 3.1 Compass program.

A type characterizes a set of values and the set of operations that are applicable to the values.

The type declaration of values together with the definition of operations given in Mini-language Typedef allow the specification of both components of a type. In programs written in statically typed languages, like Mini-language Typedef, all variables have an associated type that is specified when the variable is declared.

One of the key issues in programming is the certainty with which we can draw conclusions about a program. Consider the following declarations:

```
TODAY:   DAY_NAME;
TRUMPS:  SUIT_NAME;
COUNTER: integer;
```

It would be meaningful to have the statements

```
TODAY   := TUE;
TRUMPS  := HEARTS;
COUNTER := COUNTER + 1;
```

but not meaningful to have the statements

```
TODAY   := SPADES;    -- SPADES is not a day
TRUMPS  := TUE;       -- TUE is not a suit
COUNTER := TODAY + 1; -- Value of expression is not
                      -- an integer
```

In the last case, we have defined through an operator declaration that the result of adding an integer to a DAY_NAME is a DAY_NAME. We cannot assign a DAY_NAME value to an integer.

As a result of the use of the types DAY_NAME and SUIT_NAME, the compiler can enforce more restrictive checking than is possible with only the primitive types of a language. There is thus a greater certainty that the program is correct—there will be no violation of type properties during execution.

Enumerated Types

As mentioned earlier, an enumerated type is defined by enumerating its values. Such types can be used as freely as integers, and often with greater clarity. For example, we may declare a table itemizing the number of hours worked on each day of the week as

```
HOURS_WORKED: array[MON..FRI] of integer;
```

Furthermore, we may have a loop iterating over Monday through Friday, as in

```
for DAY := MON..SUN loop
   -- what to do for each value of DAY
end loop;
```

Notice the clarity and reliability using the enumeration type and its values instead of encoding the days of the week as integers; for instance:

```
for DAY_INDEX := 1..7 loop
   -- what to do for each value of DAY_INDEX
end loop;
```

Unless we are careful, when we come to look at the program containing this encoding in the future, we will have difficulty in remembering how we represented days. We might wonder if we started numbering the days of the week from Monday, because that is the first working day, or from Sunday, because that is what the calendar shows as the first day of the week.

Figure 3.2 shows the definition of a number of enumerated types. The use of such types can add considerably to the clarity of a program.

Defining Record Types

The type definition mechanism for array types can be readily extended to include the type definition of record structures. A simple record type definition follows:

```
type COMPLEX =
   record
      REAL: integer;
      IMAG: integer;
   end;
```

We could write operations over this type; for example:

```
operator + (C1: COMPLEX, C2: COMPLEX) => COMPLEX
   RESULT: COMPLEX;
begin
   RESULT.REAL := C1.REAL + C2.REAL;
   RESULT.IMAG := C1.IMAG + C2.IMAG;
   return RESULT;
end;
```

```
type DAY_NAME      =  (MON, TUE, WED, THU, FRI, SAT, SUN);

type COIN          =  (PENNY, NICKEL, DIME, QUARTER,
                       HALF_DOLLAR, DOLLAR);

type DIRECTION     =  (NORTH, EAST, SOUTH, WEST);

type OP_CODE       =  (ADD, SUB, MUL, LDA, STA, STZ);

type HALF_DAY      =  (AM, PM);

type FILE_STATUS   =  (OPEN, CLOSED);

type ARMY_RANK     =  (PRIVATE, CORPORAL, SERGEANT, LIEUTENANT,
                       CAPTAIN, MAJOR, COLONEL, GENERAL) ;

type CONTROL_CHAR  =  (NULL, END_OF_TRANSMISSION, ENQUIRE,
                       BELL,BACKSPACE, LINE_FEED,
CANCEL,ESCAPE);

type PEN_STATUS    =  (DOWN, UP);

type SHAPE         =  (TRIANGLE, QUADRANGLE, PENTAGON,
HEXAGON);

type DRIVING_CODE  =  (NORMAL, LIMITED, SPECIAL, VIP);

type COLOR_NAME    =  (RED, BLUE, GREEN, BROWN);
```

Figure 3.2   A sampler of enumerated types.

We could then write

```
VAL1, VAL2: COMPLEX;
...
VAL1:= VAL1 + VAL2;
```

The components of a record need not be restricted to the predefined types, such as integer, but may be any other type defined in a program. The following sequence of declarations is thus perfectly acceptable:

```
type MONTH_NAME = (JAN, FEB, MAR, APR, MAY, JUN,
                   JUL, AUG, SEP, OCT, NOV, DEC);
type YEAR_NUMBER = integer 1776..2001;
type DAY_NUMBER  = integer 1..31;
type DATE =
   record
      MONTH: MONTH_NAME;
      DAY:   DAY_NUMBER;
      YEAR:  YEAR_NUMBER;
   end;
```

This set of declarations provides the basis on which the following are built:

```
type EMPLOYEE_NUM   = integer;
type MARITAL_STATUS = (SINGLE, MARRIED, DIVORCED, WIDOWED);
type EMPLOYEE =
   record
      ID:     EMPLOYEE_NUM;
      STATUS: MARITAL_STATUS;
      BORN:   DATE;
      HIRED:  DATE;
   end;
```

Note that in the last record type definition, the two fields BORN and HIRED are actually two record components of type DATE.

Just as for other types, variables may be declared as having a record type. Example record variable declarations are

```
PERSON: EMPLOYEE;
BIRTH_DATE, TODAY: DATE;
```

Here the two variables BIRTH_DATE and TODAY have the same type. Thus, it is clear to the user that the variables have identical structure and component types.

The components of record type variables may be selected with the conventional dot notation. Thus,

```
TODAY.MONTH
```

refers to the MONTH component of TODAY. In some languages, global operators, that is, operators that apply to the entire structure, are allowed. For example, if REC1 and REC2 have the same record type,

```
(REC1 = REC2)
```

will be true only if all corresponding components in REC1 and REC2 have identical values, and

```
REC1 := REC2;
```

will assign the value of REC1 to REC2.

3.3   USER-DEFINED OPERATORS

Consider a program that is manipulating data of the type DATE, where the type DATE was defined before. Although the declaration part of the program will show that the program concerns *dates*, the executable part may contain statements such as

```
TOMORROW.DAY := TODAY.DAY + 1;
```

and much of the abstraction is lost because it is written, not in terms of dates, but in terms of fields or components of the type named DATE. It is not clear to the reader that TOMORROW gets the right value during execution; all assignments to the individual fields of TOMORROW must be inspected. If for any reason the definition of the type named DATE has to be changed, the executable part of the program must be scanned for further changes. For large programs, this process is especially unreliable.

Suppose we want to rewrite this program in a manner that better emphasizes the abstraction of a *date*. We would like to write something like

```
input TODAY;
TOMORROW := NEXT_DATE(TODAY);
output TOMORROW;
```

or

```
input TODAY;
TOMORROW := TODAY + 1;
output TOMORROW;
```

To write such a program, we need to be able to define a new operation (the function NEXT_DATE) or overload the operator "+" to add a date and an integer.

Consider the function NEXT_DATE, which takes a DATE as an argument and returns a DATE as a result. This function might read

```
NEXT_DATE: function(D: DATE) DATE;
```

```
      NEXT: DATE;
begin
   NEXT.DAY := NEXT_DAY(D);
   if (NEXT.DAY < D.DAY)
      NEXT.MONTH = NEXT_MONTH(D.MONTH);
   else
      NEXT.MONTH = D.MONTH;
   if (NEXT.MONTH < D.MONTH)
      NEXT.YEAR := D.YEAR + 1;
   else
      NEXT.YEAR := D.YEAR;
   return NEXT;
end;
```

It is only during the writing of an operation such as this that the actual structure of the type DATE needs to be defined. The operator NEXT_DATE is defined through the use of the operators NEXT_DAY and NEXT_MONTH, and the operator < is overloaded to operate on values of type MONTH_NAME.

Note: In this example, the option to define a function NEXT_DATE is not possible in Mini-language Typedef, where all new operations are defined by overloading predefined operators.

By careful programming, knowledge of a type representation can be restricted to its own operators, as indicated before. Such practice makes a program easier to understand and maintain.

Overloading Revisited

The ability to give operators new meaning can be extended to give functions and procedures new meaning. Extending the definition of an operator, function, or procedure is called *overloading.* This idea is illustrated in Figure 3.3.

Types as Abstractions

Type definition mechanisms enable the user to bring the programming environment closer to the application. The early stages of program design will likely require more effort and discipline to select the abstractions that need to be implemented. However, good type definitions promote the development of self-documenting code and security.

Mini-language Typedef embodies several of the basic ideas for a data type definition mechanism. However, the mini-language lacks some

Overloading — *Operators*

```
operator + (S1: string; S2: string) return string is
begin
   -- code to concatenate two strings
end;

operator + (S1: string; C: character) return string is
begin
   -- code to concatenate a string and a character
end;

operator + (C: character; S2: string) return string is
begin
   -- code to concatenate a character and a string
end;

operator + (R1: rectangle; R2: rectangle)
   return rectangle is
begin
   -- code to concatenate two rectangles
end;
```

Overloading — *Functions*

```
function concat (S1: string; S2: string)
   return string is
begin
   -- code to concatenate two strings
end;

function concat (S1: string; C: character)
   return string is
begin
   -- code to concatenate a string and a character
end;
```

Figure 3.3 Varieties of overloading.

```
function concat (C: character; S2: string)
   return string is
begin
   -- code to concatenate a character and a string
end;

function concat (R1: rectangle; R2: rectangle)
   return rectangle is
begin
   -- code to concatenate two rectangles
end;
```

Overloading — *Procedures*

```
procedure put (C: character) is
begin
   -- code to print a character
end;

procedure put (I: integer) is
begin
   -- code to print an integer
end;

procedure put (S: string) is
begin
   -- code to print a string
end;

procedure put (S: string) is
begin
   -- code to print a string
end;

procedure put (D: date) is
begin
   -- code to print a date
end;
```

Figure 3.3 (continued)

important features in object-oriented programming. These allow the programmer to exercise the full power of a type definition mechanism. They include the ability to define operations as part of the type definition and to make the type definition into a module that is separate from the program. These techniques are discussed in subsequent chapters.

3.4 A NOTE ON PASCAL

The general idea of defining new types, the basis for object-oriented programming, owes much to Pascal. Pascal in a sense made an historical step with its simple but powerful mechanism for defining new types. The declaration

```
type TABLE = array[1..10] of integer;
```

not only introduces a new name for a type, but it suggests a new approach to programming. This simple line is a precursor of object-oriented programming.

The model for enumerated types and subranges shown in Mini-language Typedef comes from Pascal, though the form is slightly different. Types in Pascal are defined in a special section of a program, procedure, or function, introduced by the keyword type. Some example type declarations are

```
type
   DAYNAME       = (MON, TUE, WED, THU, FRI, SAT, SUN);
   WEEKDAY       = MON..FRI;
   HOURSWORKED   = array [DAYNAME] of integer;
   TOTALRECEIPTS = record
                      DATE:   DAYNAME;
                      AMOUNT: real;
                   end;
```

The relational operators =, <>, <, >, <=, and >= are defined for enumerated types. In addition, the successor and predecessor operators, succ and pred, which give the next and previous values in an enumeration sequence, are defined. The assignment operator is defined for identical types. Pascal does not permit the user to overload any of the standard operators for use with user-defined types.

FURTHER READING

A major early work in this area [Hoare 1973] discusses simple types as well as composite types. Other key early works include [Liskov and Zilles 1974], [Guttag 1977], and [Gries and Gehani 1977].

Again, the book by J. Craig Cleaveland [Cleaveland 1986] is an excellent source work in the area of data types. The Ada 9X Rationale [Ada Rationale 1993] presents a thoughtful review of the type area.

EXERCISES

Exercise 3.1 *Multiple Choice*

Pick the answer that best fits the question.

1. A type definition
    a. allows a variable to have a specially designated type.
    b. implies a set of properties.
    c. defines a set of elements.
    d. always has a name in Mini-language Typedef.
    e. all of the above.

2. Consider Example 3.1. In this example we have the type definitions

    ```
    type HEADING = (NORTH, EAST SOUTH, WEST);
    type TURN = (RIGHT, REVERSE, LEFT);
    ```

    as well as a definition of the operator +. Also consider the expression

    ```
    D + T
    ```

    where D is of type DIRECTION and T is of type TURN. For example, if D has the value SOUTH and T has the value LEFT, the value of D + T is EAST.
    Which of the following is true?
    a. TURN is a subtype.
    b. T must be a constant.
    c. DIRECTION is a reference to a value.
    d. If D has the value SOUTH, the value of D + 2 is NORTH.
    e. None of the above.

3. In situation 2,
    a. LEFT + 1 is RIGHT.

b. NORTH + 1 is EAST.
c. NORTH cannot be the name of a variable.
d. the value of NORTH is 0.
e. the value of NORTH is 1.

4. Situation 2 is an example of
   a. abstract data types.
   b. dynamic binding.
   c. information hiding.
   d. implicit type conversion.
   e. none of the above.
   f. all of the above.

5. In Mini-language Typedef,
   a. two enumerated types can have the same identifier.
   b. an operator can have no result type.
   c. anonymous subtypes are allowed.
   d. strings are treated as arrays.
   e. none of the above.

6. In a conventional situation, + is already defined as an operator to add two integers. Which of the following operations would not be a valid overloading of the + operator?
   a. An operator to concatenate two strings.
   b. An operator to form the intersection of two sets.
   c. An operator to double two integers and return the resulting sum.
   d. An operator to print two arrays and return the value 1.
   e. An operator to add two floating-point numbers.

7. Which of the following is not really true?
   a. Overloading can be confusing.
   b. Enumeration types are usually ordered.
   c. Record types are used to represent heterogeneous entities.
   d. Dates are really integers.
   e. Mini-language Typedef is like Ada.

Exercise 3.2 *The Stack Data Type*

Define an extension to Mini-language Typedef that adds a stack structure to the base language in the same way that an array is part of the language. This definition should include the operations that are to be available in the language for the access and manipulation of stacks.

Exercise 3.3 *Enumerated Types*

In Pascal, the functions succ and pred are predefined operations that apply to enumeration values. They yield respectively the next and previous values of an enumeration value in the declared ordering. For a given enumeration type, the first value in the type definition has no predecessor, and the last value has no successor.

The following is a program fragment in an extension to Mini language Typedef. It contains the two functions for performing a computation by iterating over the days of the week:

```
DAY := MON;
while (DAY <> SAT) loop
   -- what to do for each value of DAY
   DAY := succ(DAY);
end loop;
```

If we attempt to modify this program to iterate over Monday through Sunday, a problem arises. Describe this problem. Propose changes to the language that would avoid this problem entirely.

Exercise 3.4 *Definition of Record Types*

Write down the context-free productions needed to add the record type definitions like those given in Section 3.3 to Mini-language Typedef.

Exercise 3.5 *Extensible Languages*

Opinions differ on what extensible means when applied to programming languages. At a simple level, only simple text substitution is allowed, whereas at an ambitious level, elaborate new data types and operations on them can be defined.

Describe what you feel an extensible language should offer. Aim for an intermediate level of complexity between the two extremes: simple enough for competent programmers to understand and use without heroic efforts, yet complex enough to add nontrivial power and capability to the language.

Illustrate your ideas with examples showing the syntax and semantics of your extensions. Your ideas must be implementable without recourse to magic, but do not describe implementation strategy. You may assume that the base language has a reasonable assortment of data types and control structures, that is, that one can write nontrivial programs in the base language without extending it.

Exercise 3.6 *Boolean Operators*

Consider the following definition, which corresponds to a logical "and":

```
operator * (LEFT: boolean, RIGHT: boolean) => boolean
      RESULT: boolean;
   begin
     if LEFT
        RESULT := RIGHT;
     else
        RESULT := false;
     return RESULT;
   end;
```

Under what conditions would this operator behave in the same way as the short-cut logical operator defined in Chapter 2?

CHAPTER 4

Packages and Modules

My guess is that object-oriented programming will be in the 1980's what structured programming was in the 1970's. Everyone will be in favor of it. Every manufacturer will promote his products as supporting it. Every manager will pay lip service to it. Every programmer will practice it. And no one will know just what it is.

[Rentsch 1982]
[see also Seidewitz 1991]

A program is a model of a real-world process. Because the real-world is always changing, programs are always subject to change. The modification of existing programs accounts for well over 50 percent of all software costs. A major aim of program modularization is that of containing the modifications to a program within a few modules. Modularization is rather like the idea of making a ship seaworthy by dividing the hull into watertight compartments. If the hull is damaged and starts to leak, the problem can be contained within a single compartment and the ship prevented from foundering.

With good modularization, the work of building a large program can be divided among several people, each of whom must produce part of the whole. The complexity of the program is thus reduced by dividing it into separate well-defined parts or modules. The modules must be separated so that an individual programmer is able to write one module without needing to know the internal details of another module.

To gain full advantage from modularization, the modules must be written, compiled, and, if necessary, executed separately. One of the problems of conventional Basic, Fortran, and Pascal is that there is no specific language feature for implementing modules. This makes it difficult for many people to work on a single program simultaneously.

In this chapter, we discuss the concept of a "module," or "package." This concept is one of the most powerful ideas in programming. The structure of the mini-language presented here is based on the concept of packages in Ada and modules in Modula 2.

We define here a few terms related to object-oriented programming:

Encapsulation	Grouping of essential characteristics, e.g., all about commands or all about telephone numbers.
Abstraction	Hiding of details that do not contribute to essential characteristics.
Information hiding	Restricting the visibility of an object, variable, or an operation to the implementation part of a module.
Package	A programming construct for defining collections of items.
Module	A programming construct for defining collections of items.

We use the terms module and package interchangeably.

4.1   MINI-LANGUAGE MODULES

A program in Mini-language Modules generally consists of a main part (containing variable declarations and executable statements) and a set of modules. A module, or the main part of a program, is called a "program unit" (as in Ada). The syntax of Mini-language Modules is defined in Figure 4.1. The modules and the main part are compiled separately and their object modules linked together before execution.

In both the main part and the modules, the usual assignment, loop, if, input, and output statements can all be used. Declarations in the main part define variables to be either of the primitive types boolean or integer, or of some types that are defined within modules. For example, consider the following declaration section:

```
TODAY, TOMORROW: DATE;
```

Figure 4.1   Mini-language Modules.

```
program                ::= main-part
                       [   module ]...
main-part              ::= program
                                variable-declaration...
                           begin
                                statement...
                           end ;
module                 ::= identifier : module
                                type-declaration...
                                variable-declaration...
                                operation-description...
                           implementation
                                type-declaration...
                                variable-declaration...
                                operation-algorithm...
                           end ;
variable-declaration   ::= identifier [ , identifier ]... : type ;
type                   ::= integer | boolean | string | identifier
operation-description  ::= designator: ( type [, type ]... ) [=> type ] ;
designator             ::= identifier | operator
type-declaration       ::= identifier = record
                                identifier: type ;
                                [ identifier: type ; ]...
                           end ;
operation-algorithm    ::= operation designator (identifier
                                               [, identifier ]... )
                                variable-declaration...
                           begin
                                statement...
                                [ return expression ; ]
                           end ;
statement              ::= assignment-statement | call-statement
                       |   if-statement | loop-statement
                       |   input-statement | output-statement
assignment-statement   ::= variable := expression ;
call-statement         ::= application ;
```

Figure 4.1   (continued)

if-statement	::= **if** (expression)
	if-option
	[**else**
	if-option]
if-option	::= statement | { statement... }
loop-statement	::= **while** expression **loop**
	statement...
	end loop ;
input-statement	::= **input** variable [, variable]... ;
output-statement	::= **output** expression [, expression]... ;
expression	::= operand [operator operand]
operand	::= integer | boolean | string | variable | call
	| (expression)
call	::= identifier (expression [, expression]...)
variable	::= identifier | identifier . identifier
operator	::= < | = | ≠ | > | + | − | * | **div** | **and** | **or**

```
DAY_NUMBER, MONTH_NUMBER, YEAR_NUMBER: integer;
```

Here we see a major difference between this mini-language and Mini-language Typedef in Chapter 3. In Mini-language Typedef, a type and any operations for the data type are described in the part of the program that makes use of the type. In Mini-language Modules, the main part contains no type or operator declarations; these are defined separately in corresponding modules. All that is required is that each type and each operation must be defined in a module. In the earlier case, the type DATE must be declared in some module and any operations using the type DATE must be defined in the same module or in other modules.

Modules

A module consists of two parts: a visible part and an implementation part. The visible part defines variables, types, and operations. The operations can make use of types defined by other modules in the program. The operations can manipulate values of the types being defined and perform conversions between these values and values of other types.

    The implementation part contains the statements that perform each operation defined in the visible part.

The visible part of the ALL_ABOUT_DATES module might, for example, consist of the following descriptions:

```
ALL_ABOUT_DATES: module
    type DATE = record
                    MONTH: integer;
                    DAY:   integer;
                    YEAR:  integer;
                 end;
    SET_DATE:     (integer, integer, integer) => DATE;
    DATE_YEAR:    (DATE) => integer;
    DATE_MONTH:   (DATE) => integer;
    DATE_DAY:     (DATE) => integer;
    +:            (DATE, integer) => DATE;
```

These definitions show the names of the operations, the types of their parameters, and the type of their returned value, if any. Thus, the type of SET_DATE is defined as

```
integer, integer, integer => DATE
```

This function is intended to take three integers, representing day, month, and year numbers, and compose them to form a date. The functions DATE_YEAR, DATE_MONTH, and DATE_DAY provide conversions in the opposite direction. The operation + takes a DATE value and an integer value, representing an elapsed number of days, and returns a new DATE value.

With this information, it is possible to write the statements that make use of the preceding functions to construct the complete main part of the program, for example:

```
program
    TODAY, TOMORROW: DATE;
    DAY_NUM, MONTH_NUM, YEAR_NUM: integer;
begin
    input DAY_NUM, MONTH_NUM, YEAR_NUM;
    TODAY      := SET_DATE(DAY_NUM, MONTH_NUM, YEAR_NUM);
    TOMORROW   := TODAY + 1;
    DAY_NUM    := TOMORROW.DAY;
    MONTH_NUM := TOMORROW.MONTH;
    YEAR_NUM   := TOMORROW.YEAR;
    output DAY_NUM, MONTH_NUM, YEAR_NUM;
end;
```

This section of the program is written separately from the ALL_ABOUT_DATES module.

The implementation part of a module provides the missing details that are required to make the complete program workable. It consists of the variable and type declarations describing internal values, as well as the actual algorithms for the operations defined in the visible part.

The operation algorithms are written in the style of the operators in Mini-language Typedef. Each operation has a set of named parameters of a type that is defined in the visible part. Parameter values are passed by value so that none of the operations can have any side effects. In addition, an operation may make use of local variables that are declared within the operation. The types of these local variables can be defined by other type modules.

As an example of an operation algorithm, the SET_DATE operation might be written as

```
operation SET_DATE (DAY_NUM, MONTH_NUM, YEAR_NUM) => DATE
   CONVERTED_DATE: DATE;
begin
   . . .  -- code to check validity of parameter values
   CONVERTED_DATE.DAY   := DAY_NUM;
   CONVERTED_DATE.MONTH := MONTH_NUM;
   CONVERTED_DATE.YEAR  := YEAR_NUM;
   return CONVERTED_DATE;
end;
```

An alternative way in which dates might be represented is

```
DATE = record
          DECADE_DAY: integer;
       end;
```

where the field DECADE_DAY contains the number of days that have elapsed since January 1, 1990. To make this change, the program would need to be examined to find all places that refer to the fields of values of type DATE.

The remainder of Mini-language Modules is in the style of the previous mini-languages. The arithmetic operations include div to provide integer division, and the class of operands include the application of an operation to a set of arguments.

Notice that a module need not be about a single subject or a single type. The module

```
MISC_1: module
    constant PI = 3.14159
    type BUFFER = ...
type PAGE   = ...
    type DATE   = ...
    procedure PRINT_HEADER;
end;
```

for example, is valid.

Example

Example 4.1 shows a complete Mini-language Modules program. It performs operations on complex numbers represented by the data type COMPLEX. Notice that Mini-languge Modules allow us to use symbols, such as + and =, to overload operators as is done in Mini-language Typedef. The type COMPLEX is defined in a module, where complex numbers are represented as records with two elements, REAL and IMAG. These correspond to the real and imaginary parts of the complex numbers. The module provides operations for converting between pairs of integers and complex numbers, and selecting the real and imaginary parts. The module also provides operations for testing complex numbers for equality, adding complex numbers, and multiplying complex numbers.

4.2 PACKAGES AND MODULES

The idea of packages of subroutines that provide a particular kind of facility have been available in programming since the early days. In fact, packages for matrix arithmetic and mathematical functions were available before the advent of high-level programming languages. The ability to construct modules easily as a part of normal program writing is an outgrowth of this idea.

Packages and modules have many uses. Two simple Ada-like examples are given in Figure 4.2. Here the first package, named COMMON_CONSTANTS, is simply a grouping of declarations giving the names of various constants. This kind of package can ensure that programmers writing other modules use the same names for these constants, thus ensuring both uniformity and, presumably, a greater program readability.

The second example in Figure 4.2 is a package called SIMPLE_I_O. This package contains a constant, two types, a variable, two functions, and four

```
program
   X, Y, Z: COMPLEX;
   R_VAL, I_VAL: integer;
begin
   input R_VAL, I_VAL;
   X := SET_CPLX(R_VAL, I_VAL);
   input R_VAL, I_VAL;
   Y := SET_CPLX(R_VAL, I_VAL);
   if (X = Y)
      Z := X + Y;
   else
      Z := X * Y;
   R_VAL := REAL_PART(Z);
   I_VAL := IMAG_PART(Z);
   output R_VAL, I_VAL;
end;


COMPLEX_NUMBERS: module
   COMPLEX = record
                REAL: integer;
                IMAG: integer;
             end record;

   SET_CPLX:   (integer, integer) => COMPLEX;
   =:          (COMPLEX, COMPLEX) => boolean;
   +:          (COMPLEX, COMPLEX) => COMPLEX;
   *:          (COMPLEX, COMPLEX) => COMPLEX;
   REAL_PART:  (COMPLEX) => integer;
   IMAG_PART:  (COMPLEX) => integer;

implementation
   operation SET_CPLX (R_PART, I_PART) is
      RESULT: COMPLEX;
   begin
      RESULT.REAL := R_PART;
      RESULT.IMAG := I_PART;
      return RESULT;
   end;
```

Example 4.1 Mini-language Modules program.

```
operation = (A, B) is
   RESULT: boolean;
begin
   if (A.REAL = B.REAL)
      if (A.IMAG = B.IMAG)
         RESULT := true;
      else
         RESULT := false;
   else
      RESULT := false;
   return RESULT;
end;

operation + (A, B) is
   RESULT: COMPLEX;
begin
   RESULT.REAL := A.REAL + B.REAL;
   RESULT.IMAG := A.IMAG + B.IMAG;
   return RESULT;
end;

operation * (A, B) is
    RESULT: COMPLEX;
begin
   RESULT.REAL := A.REAL*B.REAL - A.IMAG*B.IMAG;
   RESULT.IMAG := A.REAL*B.IMAG + A.IMAG*B.REAL;
   return RESULT;
end;

operation REAL_PART (CPLX_VAL) is
 begin
   return CPLX_VAL.REAL;
 end;

operation IMAG_PART (CPLX_VAL) is
 begin
   return CPLX_VAL.IMAG;
 end;
end;
```

Example 4.1   (continued)

```
package COMMON_CONSTANTS is
   PAGE_SIZE = 66;
   LINES_PER_PAGE = 54;
   LEFT_MARGIN = 15;
   RIGHT_MARGIN = 10;

   BUFFER_SIZE = 200;
   MAX_SYMBOL_LENGTH = 32;

   COMMAND_CHAR = "@"
   BLANK = ' ';
end;


package SIMPLE_I_O is
   constant LINE_SIZE = 120;
   type BUFFER = array [1..LINE_SIZE] of character;
   type LINE_INFO =
      record
         LINE:    BUFFER;
         LENGTH:  integer;
      end;

   NEXT_INPUT_CHAR: character;

   function MORE_DATA (F: in_file) return boolean;
   function MORE_ON_LINE (F: in_file) return boolean;

   procedure GET_CHAR (C: out character);
   procedure GET_LINE (L: out line_info);

   procedure PRINT_MARGIN (MARGIN: in string);
   procedure PRINT_TEXT (LINE: in line_info);
end;

package body SIMPLE_I_O is
   . . .
end;
```

Figure 4.2 Sample packages.

procedures. All of them relate to input and output. They are grouped together presumably so that all the visible features relating to input-output occur in this single package. The package body completes the definition of the functions and procedures given in the visible part. This package represents a common scenario for using modules and packages in programming.

The division of a program into separate modules or packages has a number of advantages:

- *Reduction in complexity:* Because the program has been reduced into small pieces, the complexity of each piece can be made much smaller than the program as a whole. The COMPLEX_NUMBERS module reduces the complexity of the main part of the program by removing the details of performing complex arithmetic.

- *Ease of team programming:* A large program is almost always the work of a team of programmers. If the program is split into well-defined modules with clear interfaces, the members of the team can work individually on different modules without requiring a great deal of communication. A large number of the errors in software can be attributed to failures in communication among the programmers.

- *Improved maintainability:* The principles suggested in [Parnas 1971] suggest that a program be split into modules, each of which "hides" design decisions. Examples of these decisions are the format of input data or the internal representation of data values. If this is done, it is likely that changes to the program's specifications will result in modifications to the program that are localized to very few modules.

- *Reusability of code:* By splitting programs into modules, it is likely that the solution to one problem can incorporate modules that were part of the solution of another. For example, the COMPLEX_NUMBERS module shown in the previous section could be used for other programs that require complex integer arithmetic.

- *Project management:* A modular program is easier for a manager to control. The programming of the modules can be assigned to the programmers according to their individual abilities. Control of the project is easier because the modules are visible and their completion represents milestones in the project's progress.

Mini-language Modules brings up a small but interesting point. In the interface specification for the module, the names of the parameters for the operations are not given. Rather, just the type names for the parameters and the type of the result, if any, are given with each defined operation. This is in line with the fact that the parameter names normally do not need to be known by any other program unit making use of the module.

We note that the package concept is so broad that, if not used properly, a package can also complicate program readability. A package can become so cumbersome and so diffuse in its purposes that any gain made because things are grouped together begins to disintegrate.

We also note that the packages of Figure 4.2 are not "object-oriented." Neither package describes a single kind of object. The first package is a collection of miscellaneous objects. The second package is a collection of routines.

4.3 ENCAPSULATION AND ABSTRACTION

The concept of packages or modules brings up a number of key issues related to programming in general and to object-oriented programming in particular.

The first of these is *encapsulation*. This is the basic idea behind a package or module. That is, we group all of the information about a single concept into a single syntactic unit. In Modula-2, this is called a *module.* In Ada, this is called a *package.* As an example consider Figure 4.3. Here we see the definition of a constant, a type, and three procedures. All of these constructs relate to the single notion of a stack of integers. The items are grouped into a single syntactic unit, here the package.

Next consider Figure 4.4. This is a revised version of Figure 4.3. Here we add the notion of *abstraction.* In this figure, the constant, the type, and the three procedure headers are grouped into a single unit. This is the abstraction. For the procedures, only a header is given. A separate unit, the package body, defines the actual code for each of the procedures.

In this way, we "abstract" out the essential properties of a stack. In Ada, this grouping is called the *visible part* of a package. This concept is a powerful one. For what it means "to abstract out essential ingredients" is precisely a listing of constants, types, functions, and procedures. This is the information another program or program unit needs to know in order to utilize the concepts embodied in the given package. In Figure 4.3, for example, the implementation of the stack is of no consequence to the user.

Although use of functions and procedures can provide good support

```
package STACK_PKG is
   const
      MAX_STACK_SIZE := 100;
   type
      stack_structure is record
         CONTENTS: array [1..MAX_STACK_SIZE] of integer;
         SIZE: integer;
      end;

   procedure INITIALIZE_STACK (S: stack_structure) is
   begin
      S.SIZE := 0;
   end;

   procedure PUSH (S: stack_structure; ITEM: integer) is
   begin
      if (S.SIZE < MAX_STACK_SIZE) then
         S.SIZE := S.SIZE + 1;
         S.CONTENTS[S.SIZE] := ITEM;
      else
         -- Handle full stack error
      end if;
   end;

   procedure POP (S: stack_structure; ITEM: integer) is
      var
         ITEM : integer;
   begin
      if (S.SIZE /= 0) then
         ITEM := S.CONTENTS[S.SIZE];
         S.SIZE := S.SIZE - 1;
      else
         --  Handle empty stack error
      end if;
   end;
end;
```

Figure 4.3 Encapsulation.

```
package STACK_PKG is
   const MAX_STACK_SIZE := 100;
   type
      stack_structure is record
         CONTENTS: array [1..MAX_STACK_SIZE] of integer;
         SIZE: integer;
      end;

   procedure INITIALIZE_STACK (S: stack_structure);
   procedure PUSH (S: stack_structure; ITEM: integer);
   procedure POP  (S: stack_structure; ITEM: integer);
end;

package body STACK_PKG is

   procedure INITIALIZE_STACK (S: stack_structure) is
   begin
      S.SIZE := 0;
   end;

   procedure PUSH (S: stack_structure; ITEM: integer) is
   begin
      if (S.SIZE < MAX_STACK_SIZE) then
         S.SIZE := S.SIZE + 1;
         S.CONTENTS[S.SIZE] := ITEM;
      else
         -- Handle full stack error
      end if;
   end;

   procedure POP (S: stack_structure; ITEM: integer) is
   begin
      if (S.SIZE /= 0) then
         ITEM := S.CONTENTS[S.SIZE];
         S.SIZE := S.SIZE - 1;
      else
         --  Handle empty stack error
      end if;
   end;
end;
```

Figure 4.4 Abstraction.

for abstractions, it does not guarantee the integrity of these abstractions. In the DATE example given earlier, nothing prevents a main program from accessing the fields of a DATE and changing them arbitrarily. This may be convenient, but it may also lead to troubles. For instance, the main program could set a date variable to the thirty-first day of February, which is not a valid date. Furthermore, it is not known how the operations over a date would behave on invalid dates, because they were written with real dates in mind. Programming errors of this kind can be difficult to correct. Thus, some safeguards are needed to preserve the integrity of these abstractions.

Similarly, in the abstraction of the stacks, we see a certain anomaly. This is that the type name stack_structure is needed in order to declare items of type stack, but the actual record structure defining the type is of no consequence to a programmer using the package. In fact, the abstraction would be better if the record structure were not visible to another program unit. The record structure is only needed by the package body in order to make its implementation work internally.

One solution to this problem is the idea of private types in Ada. This is a powerful idea and is illustrated in Figure 4.5. The first type declaration specifies that the type is private. Later, in the same declarative part, there is the actual full type declaration of the type stack_structure. The appearance of this type declaration after the keyword "private" means that any program or program unit using the package may not make use of this information.

Ideally, the full type declaration for the type stack_structure would appear in the package body and only the type name would appear in the visible part. This poses difficulties for an implementation. It should be possible to compile the visible part of the package separately from the package body. Only the visible part need be made available to other program units. This means that another unit would be compiled knowing only the type name, and not knowing the actual type declaration for the type stack_structure. Conceivably, the type stack_structure could be implemented as a special kind of array, or even with pointers. The fact that it is a record type here would not then be known when other program units are compiled.

The Ada compromise to this solution is to include the actual type declaration in the visible part, but in a separate section beginning with the key word private. This means that the programmer may not make use of the type information in the private section, but the compiler may.

```
package STACK_PKG is
   const MAX_STACK_SIZE := 100;
   type stack_structure is private;

   procedure INITIALIZE_STACK (S: stack_structure);
   procedure PUSH (S: stack_structure; ITEM integer);
   procedure POP  (S: stack_structure; ITEM: integer);
private
   type stack_structure is record
      CONTENTS: array [1..MAX_STACK_SIZE] of integer;
      SIZE: integer;
   end;
end;

package body STACK_PKG is
   procedure INITIALIZE_STACK (S: stack_structure) is
   begin
      S.SIZE := 0;
   end;

   procedure PUSH (S: stack_structure; ITEM: integer) is
   begin
      if (S.SIZE < MAX_STACK_SIZE) then
         S.SIZE := S.SIZE + 1;
         S.CONTENTS[S.SIZE] := ITEM;
      else
         -- Handle full stack error
      end if;
   end;

procedure POP (S: stack_structure; ITEM: integer) is
   begin
      if (S.SIZE /= 0) then
         ITEM := S.CONTENTS[S.SIZE];
         S.SIZE := S.SIZE - 1;
      else
         -- Handle empty stack error
      end if;
   end;
end;
```

Figure 4.5 Private types.

4.4 INFORMATION HIDING

We can take yet another step in our sequence of stack packages and remove the stack itself as a parameter of the procedures. We can make the actual stack local to the package body. This gives the situation illustrated in Figure 4.6. Here, the type declaration for the `stack_structure` also goes directly in the package body, for the stack is not even visible to the user of the stack package. For the user, the stack thus becomes a mental object. It does not have a direct presence as far as the user of the package is concerned. This phenomenon is a version of information hiding. In this case, we actually hide the stack itself inside the package body.

Figure 4.6 also contains another idea: automatic initialization of a module. The end of the package contains an executable part that is invoked when the module itself is initialized. This executable part is called an "initialization part." In Figure 4.6, the initialization part is a single statement, an assignment of 0 to the local variable `SIZE`; this statement is executed before the package can be used.

The version as presented in Figure 4.6 has one clear drawback. Only one stack can be created with this package. Because the stack itself is local to the package body, only one stack can come into existence. A program that needs two stacks cannot use this particular version.

In Ada, this drawback can be removed by declaring the package to be "generic." Generic (or parameterized) packages have unspecified components denoted by parameters. Each time a new stack is needed, a value for the parameter is provided and a new "generic instantiation" is made to create a new stack.

Nevertheless, the approach via generics is not a complete solution to the issue. We wish the new types to behave like the built-in types. In particular, we wish to define procedures and functions over values of the type, allow operators over these values to be defined, define what assignment means, declare arrays with values of the new type, and so on. Moreover, generally, we wish to have many objects of a type. These issues lead us to the next chapter.

4.5 SEPARATE COMPILATION

Although the construction of a large program is made easier by splitting it into modules, the full advantages of this will not be realized unless the individual programmers are able to compile and test these parts before

```
package STACK_PKG is
   procedure INITIALIZE_STACK;
   procedure PUSH (ITEM: integer);
   procedure POP  (ITEM: integer);
end;


package body STACK_PKG is
   const MAX_STACK_SIZE := 100;
   type stack_structure is record
      CONTENTS: array [1..MAX_STACK_SIZE] of integer;
      SIZE: integer;
   end;
   var
      S: stack_structure;

   procedure PUSH (ITEM: integer) is
   begin
      if (S.SIZE < MAX_STACK_SIZE) then
         S.SIZE := S.SIZE + 1;
         S.CONTENTS[S.SIZE] := ITEM;
      else
         -- Handle full stack error
      end if;
   end;

   procedure POP (ITEM: integer) is
   begin
      if (S.SIZE /= 0) then
         ITEM := S.CONTENTS[S.SIZE];
         S.SIZE := S.SIZE - 1;
      else
         --  Handle empty stack error
      end if;
   end;

begin
   S.SIZE := 0;
end;
```

Figure 4.6 Information hiding.

incorporation into the complete program. Separate compilation of modules has some implications for language design. This is because in the course of compiling one module, information about another module is required in order to ensure consistency.

There are two major ways in which this information can be made available to the compiler:

1. The programmer can provide the name of a file that contains the information that is required by the compiler. Examples of this occur in C through `#include`.

2. The compiler can obtain the information from the program library. In the case of Mini-language Modules, the compiler is able to access the interface specifications for the named items directly.

In the second method, the supporting compiler would obtain the interface specifications from the referenced modules during compilation. The visible part can be written *before* completing the operation algorithms, which can be left as stubs. This technique matches the top-down programming method. As generally understood, this means that programs are coded from the highest level downward. During the coding of one level, only the interfaces with the next lower level are defined. The coding of the lower level is only undertaken when the higher level has been completed.

Some method must be devised to identify which modules are needed for compilation of a unit. The module names could be provided at the time of compilation. A better solution could be achieved by adding a clause to each unit identifying the names of the needed modules. In Mini-language Modules, we could add a construct such as

```
uses ALL_ABOUT_DATES;
program
    ...
end;
```

This is the method used in Ada.

4.6 MODULA-2 AND ADA

Modula-2

Modula-2 [Wirth 1983] is a descendent from Pascal. The unit that is processed by the compiler is called a *compilation unit*, or *module*. The main part of the program consists of a main module. The units of data abstraction consist of separately compiled modules called *definition* and *implementation modules*.

Any identifiers that are to be imported from outside a module must be named in an import list, together with the name of the module from which they are to be imported. Any identifiers that are to be made available for reference outside a module must be named on an export list. The main module may not have an export list. Only the name of an exported type is known outside a module; its representation is not exported. The only way in which a type defined by a module can be manipulated is through exported procedures.

The major purpose of a module is to limit scope and to hide the information about the representation of a type. The definition module specifies the names and properties of types that are relevant to other modules that import from it. The implementation module contains local variables and operations that need not be known by the importing module. The following is an incomplete example based on one in [Wirth 1983] and is designed to give the flavor of type definition in Modula-2:

```
definition module BUFFER;
    export PUT, GET, NONEMPTY, NONFULL;
    var NONEMPTY, NONFULL: boolean;
    procedure GET(X: cardinal);
    procedure PUT(var X: cardinal);
end BUFFER;
```

This shows two functions that can used to access a buffer and two variables that can be referenced to test whether it is full or empty. This corresponds closely to the specification part of a type module in Mini-language Modules. One difference is that in Modula-2, the names of the parameters are exported, whereas in the mini-language they are kept hidden. The corresponding implementation module is

```
implementation module BUFFER;
    const n = 100;
    var
        IN, OUT: [0..n-1];
        N: [1..n];
        BUF: array[0..n-1];
    procedure PUT(X: cardinal);
    begin
```

```
package D is
   type DATE is private;
   function NEXT_DATE(D: DATE) return DATE;
private
   type DATE is
      record
         -- internal structure of a date that is
         -- kept hidden from the user by the module
      end record;
end;

package body D is
   -- local declarations and types
   function NEXT_DATE(D: DATE) return DATE is
      ...
   end;
   -- definition of other operations
begin
   -- code to initialize data abstractions
end;
```

Figure 4.7   Sketch of an Ada package.

```
   if N < n then
      BUF[IN]    := X;
      IN         := (IN + 1) mod n;
      N          := N + 1;
      NONFULL    := N < n;
      NONEMPTY := true
   end PUT;
   procedure GET(X: cardinal);
      . . .
   end GET;
begin
   N          := 0;
   IN         := 0;
   OUT        := 0;
   NONEMPTY := false;
   NONFULL  := true;
end BUFFER;
```

The statements at the bottom of the module are initialization code that is invoked when an object of type BUFFER is created.

invoked when an object of type BUFFER is created.

Ada

The Ada facility for data abstraction is the package.

For the flavor of the Ada package, consider Figure 4.7, where the type DATE is sketched as an Ada package. The only items that may be known outside of the package are declared in the module header, in the span of the text between the keywords package and private, that is, the type name DATE and the fact that the operator NEXT_DATE takes a DATE value and returns a DATE value. Note that the internal representation of type DATE is kept private to the package. A user cannot make use of the fact that a date may be represented by a record structure and cannot access any field of a DATE.

FURTHER   READING

The paradigm for modules or packages is most prevalent in Modula-2 and the design of the package facility in Ada. The philosophy behind Modula-2 is described in [Wirth 1983] and the rationale for the design of Ada is given in [Ichbiah et al. 1979].

EXERCISES

Exercise 4.1 *Multiple Choice*

Pick the answer that best fits the question.

1.   The declarations

```
void pop (char);
void push(char);
```

to declare operations for a stack of characters are an example of
a.   parameterized types.
b.   inheritance.
c.   data hiding.
d.   polymorphism.
e.   none of the above.

2.   Consider the following fragment from a Mini-language Modules program:

```
program
```

```
begin
    input DAY_NUM, MONTH_NUM, YEAR_NUM;
    TODAY      := SET_DATE(DAY_NUM, MONTH_NUM, YEAR_NUM);
    TOMORROW   := TODAY + 1;
    . . .
```

Which of the following is not necessarily true?
a. SET_DATE must return an object of type DATE.
b. The type DATE is defined as a record type.
c. The operator + must be overloaded.
d. DAY_NUM and MONTH_NUM have the same type.
e. The value of MONTH_NUM is greater than 0.

3. In Mini-language Modules,
    a. two types can be defined in a visible part of a module.
    b. modules can have local variables.
    c. the symbol "," cannot be a designator.
    d. overloading of operators is allowed.
    e. all of the above.

4. Which of the following is not true of a module?
    a. There can be many user-defined types.
    b. There can be global variables.
    c. There can be no procedures.
    d. It can be run in parallel with other modules.
    e. It can overload operators.

5. A private type is
    a. a type with no name.
    b. a hidden enumeration type.
    c. a type that is used only in the package defining it.
    d. a type whose definition is not visible outside the package defining it.
    e. none of the above.

6. The primary function that a module provides is
    a. dynamic binding.
    b. encapsulation.
    c. polymorphism.
    d. type declarations.
    e. constructors.

7. Which of the following is not significantly enhanced by modules?
    a. Team programming.
    b. Modularity.

c. Program maintenance.
d. Software tools.
e. Software design.

Exercise 4.2 *Queues*

Write a package for handling queues. Use the same Ada-like notation of Example 4.6, and use information hiding to hide the representation of the queue.

Exercise 4.3 *Sets*

From the programming language point of view, a set is a data aggregate that contains an *unordered* collection of *distinct* values. This is in contrast to a single-dimensioned array, which is a data aggregate that contains an ordered collection of values, some of which may be repeated.

Describe the visible part of a module that would define sets. To do this, you will have to decide on the operations on sets that will have to be defined. Typically, these will include a membership test, insertion and deletion of single values, and the standard mathematical set operations.

Exercise 4.4 *Error Handling*

In Section 4.1, the example of the data type DATE is sketched. Mention is made that the SET_DATE function checks that the values of the three integers representing day, month, and year number are consistent. However, nothing is said about what should be done if an inconsistency is found. Propose how this should be handled and outline a new module, perhaps including extra operations.

Exercise 4.5 *Facilities for Separate Compilation*

Pick a language on your system that provides for separate compilation. Write a two-to five-page "user manual" describing only the facilities for separate compilation.

CHAPTER 5

Objects and Abstract Data Types

"Types are not sets."

[James H. Morris 1973]

"Class design is type design."

[Scott Meyers 1992]

We now turn to a significant step in achieving object-oriented programming. We approach this step again through a mini-language. This mini-language is similar to Mini-language Modules introduced in the previous chapter. There is a small but *very* significant difference, which we believe highlights the essence of object-oriented programming. Here a module *only* describes a given class of objects. The modules are called *type* modules because the purpose of the module is to define a type as presented earlier. The definition of type modules also follows the object-oriented notions of *class* and object.

These terms are especially relevant to this chapter:

Object-Oriented A perspective of classes and things, i.e., objects and nouns.

Member A procedure or function defined as one of the
Function operations for a type.

Abstract Data Type	A type whose representation is not available to the user.
Class	A programming language construct similar to a module. The module itself is the type.
Instance	An object, i.e., a member of a class.

5.1 MINI-LANGUAGE OBJECTS

A program in Mini-language Objects consists of a main part (containing the variable declarations and executable statements) and a set of *type* modules. Each type module implements a single, user-defined data type used in the main part. If the main part uses only primitive types, no type modules are given. The syntax of Mini-language Objects is defined in Figure 5.1.

In both the main part and the type modules, the usual assignment, loop, if, input, and output statements can all be used. Declarations in the main part define variables to be either of the primitive boolean or integer types, or of some types that are defined by type modules of the same name. Consider, for example, the following declaration section:

```
TODAY, TOMORROW: DATE;
DAY_NUMBER, MONTH_NUMBER, YEAR_NUMBER: integer;
```

Here the type DATE must be defined by a type module named DATE. There must be a type module describing each (nonprimitive) type being used. The type modules and the main part are compiled separately and linked together before execution.

Type Modules

A type module consists of two parts: a visible part and an implementation part. The visible part defines operations for the type. The operations can make use of types defined by other modules in the program. The operations can manipulate values of the type being defined and perform conversions between these values and values of other types. The implementation part contains the actual representation of values of the type and the statements that perform the operations defined in the interface specification.

The visible part of the type module DATE might, for example, consist of the following descriptions:

Figure 5.1   Mini-language Objects.

```
program                 ::= main-part
                            [ type-module ]...

main-part               ::= program
                                variable-declaration...
                            begin
                                statement...
                            end ;
type-module             ::= identifier : type module
                                operation-description...
                            implementation
                                type-representation
                                variable-declaration...
                                operation-algorithm...
                            end ;
variable-declaration    ::= identifier [ , identifier ]... : type ;
type                    ::= integer | boolean | string | identifier
operation-description   ::= designator: (type [ , type ]... )[ => type ] ;
designator              ::= identifier | " operator "
record-type             ::= record
                                identifier : type ;
                                [ identifier : type ; ]...
                            end
type-representation     ::= identifier = type ;
                        |   identifier = record-type ;
operation-algorithm     ::= operation designator (identifier
                                                    [ , identifier ]... ) is
                                variable-declaration...
                            begin
                                statement...
                            [ return expression ; ]
                            end ;
statement               ::= assignment-statement | call-statement
                        |   if-statement | loop-statement
                        |   input-statement | output-statement
assignment-statement    ::= variable := expression ;
call-statement          ::= application ;
```

Figure 5.1 (continued)

if-statement	::= **if** (expression)
	if-option
	[**else**
	if-option]
if-option	::= statement | { statement... }
loop-statement	::= **while** expression **loop**
	statement...
	end loop ;
input-statement	::= **input** variable [, variable]... ;
output-statement	::= **output** expression [, expression]... ;
expression	::= operand [operator operand]
operand	::= integer | boolean | string | variable | call
	| (expression)
call	::= identifier (expression [, expression]...)
variable	::= identifier | identifier . identifier]...
operator	::= < | = | ≠ | > | + | - | * | **div** | **and** | **or**

```
DATE: type module
   SET_DATE:     (integer, integer, integer) => DATE;
   DATE_YEAR:    (DATE) => integer;

DATE_MONTH:  (DATE) => integer;
   DATE_DAY:     (DATE) => integer;
   +:            (DATE, integer) => DATE;
end;
```

This module is similar to the ALL_ABOUT_DATES module in the previous chapter; in this mini-language, however, the name of the module is precisely the name of the type DATE itself, and no type definition is given in the visible part to describe the representation of dates. The visible part of the program contains no details of how DATE values are represented.

The implementation part of a module provides the missing details that are required to make the complete program workable. It consists of the representation of the type for which the module is defined, variable and type declarations describing internal values, and the actual algorithms for the operations defined in the interface specification. The operation algorithms have the same form as in Mini-language Modules. The types of local variables can be defined by other type modules.

Note that an implementation part may well contain operation descriptions whose parameters are of the type being defined by the module.

The remainder of Mini-language Objects is in the style of the previous mini-languages. The arithmetic operators include div for integer division, and the operands in an expression include the application of an operation to a list of arguments.

Example

Figure 5.2 shows a complete Mini-language Objects program. It performs operations on complex numbers and makes use of symbols, such as + and =, to overload operators, as is done in Mini-languge Modules and Mini-language Typedef. Here the type COMPLEX is, in fact, the name of the module. The representation of the type is defined in the implementation part of the type module, where complex numbers are represented as records with two elements, REAL and IMAG.

As mentioned in the previous chapter, an alternative type module for COMPLEX might have an internal representation of the values using polar coordinates. To do this would probably require a new type ANGLE and a set of operations including the trigonometric functions. These could be provided in a separate type module. Here, however, these changes could be made *without* altering the interface specification for COMPLEX. Thus, any program that uses the type COMPLEX would not need to be changed.

5.2 FULL OBJECTS

We return to our stack example given in the previous chapter and recast this example as a series of versions. Each of these versions uses a type module to define the type STACK.

The first version, Figure 5.3, falls in line with the version in Chapter 4; the major change is that STACK is now the name of the type module, reflecting the point that the entire purpose of the type module is to define a single type. Given the definitions of Figure 5.3, a programmer could write a program declaring different stack objects; for example, one might see declarations like

```
S1, S2: STACK;
```

```
program
   X, Y, Z: COMPLEX;
   R_VAL, I_VAL: integer;
begin
   input R_VAL, I_VAL;
   X := SET_CPLX(R_VAL, I_VAL);
   input R_VAL, I_VAL;
   Y := SET_CPLX(R_VAL, I_VAL);
   if (X = Y)
      Z := X + Y;
   else
      Z := X - Y;
   R_VAL := REAL_PART(Z);
   I_VAL := IMAG_PART(Z);
   output R_VAL, I_VAL;
end;

COMPLEX: type module
   SET_CPLX:  (integer, integer) => COMPLEX;
   =:         (COMPLEX, COMPLEX) => boolean;
   +:         (COMPLEX, COMPLEX) => COMPLEX;
   -:         (COMPLEX, COMPLEX) => COMPLEX;
   REAL_PART: (COMPLEX) => integer;
   IMAG_PART: (COMPLEX) => integer;

implementation
   COMPLEX = record
                REAL: integer;
                IMAG: integer;
             end record;

   operation SET_CPLX (R_PART, I_PART) is
      RESULT: COMPLEX;
   begin
      RESULT.REAL := R_PART;
      RESULT.IMAG := I_PART;
      return RESULT;
   end;
```

Figure 5.2 Mini-language Objects program.

```
operation = (A, B) is
   RESULT: boolean;
begin
   if (A.REAL = B.REAL)
      if (A.IMAG = B.IMAG)
         RESULT := true;
      else
         RESULT := false;
   else
      RESULT := false;
   return RESULT;
end;

operation + (A, B) is
   RESULT: COMPLEX;
begin
   RESULT.REAL := A.REAL + B.REAL;
   RESULT.IMAG := A.IMAG + B.IMAG;
   return RESULT;
end;

operation * (A, B) is
    RESULT: COMPLEX;
begin
   RESULT.REAL := A.REAL*B.REAL - A.IMAG*B.IMAG;
   RESULT.IMAG := A.REAL*B.IMAG + A.IMAG*B.REAL;
   return RESULT;
end;

operation REAL_PART (CPLX_VAL) is
begin
   return CPLX_VAL.REAL;
end;

operation IMAG_PART (CPLX_VAL) is
begin
   return CPLX_VAL.IMAG;
end;
```

Figure 5.2   (continued)

Here the programmer would introduce two stack structures called S1 and S2. They could be manipulated using the procedures PUSH and POP given in the type module, provided that they were initialized with a call to the procedure INITIALIZE_STACK.

Figure 5.4 introduces a major concept. This is the idea that objects have "states." What does this mean? It means that a type module defining a class of objects may need to keep internal information about the status of an object in order for the behavior of the procedures, functions, and operators to work correctly. In our case, Figure 5.4, we simply keep an internal variable SIZE. We say that the value of SIZE is a part of the "state" of the object. We also say that SIZE is an *instance variable* for an object of type STACK.

In Figure 5.4 the type module body contains an executable part, which is given at the end of the module body and which is invoked each time a stack is *declared*. In Figure 5.3, the initialization part is a single statement

```
SIZE := 0;
```

Here the size of S is initialized to be zero. The statement must be executed before any stack object can be declared.

Figure 5.5 presents yet another version. This version makes use of information hiding, where the stack itself is maintained within the module body. Stack variables have disappeared from the parameter lists of the procedures PUSH and POP. The value of the stack in a way becomes part of the state of the object. Thus, the variable S also becomes an *instance variable* for objects of the type STACK.

The information hiding in Figure 5.5 brings up a key point. Consider the declaration

```
S1: stack;
```

in the main program. This introduces a stack variable called S1. In order to push a value onto the stack, a new notation is needed. Typically, a dot notation is used. For example, we may see a statement like

```
S1.PUSH(5);
```

This statement pushes the value 5 onto stack S1. Similarly, we may see a statement like

```
S1.POP(NEW_ITEM);
```

This statement obtains the value from the top of stack S1 and puts the value

```
STACK: type module is
   const
      MAX_STACK_SIZE := 100;

   procedure INITIALIZE_STACK (S: STACK);
   procedure PUSH (S: STACK; ITEM: integer);
   procedure POP  (S: STACK; ITEM: integer);
end;

STACK: type module body is
   type
      STACK is
         record
            CONTENTS: array [1..MAX_STACK_SIZE] of integer;
            SIZE: integer;
         end;

   procedure INITIALIZE_STACK (S: STACK) is
   begin
      S.SIZE := 0;
   end;

   procedure PUSH (S: STACK; ITEM: integer) is
   begin
      if (S.SIZE < MAX_STACK_SIZE) then
         S.SIZE := S.SIZE + 1;
         S.CONTENTS[S.SIZE] := ITEM;
      else
         -- Handle full stack error
      end if;
   end;

   procedure POP (S: STACK; ITEM: integer) is
   begin
      if (S.SIZE /= 0) then
         ITEM := S.CONTENTS[S.SIZE];
         S.SIZE := S.SIZE - 1;
      else
         --  Handle empty stack error
      end if;
   end;
end;
```

Figure 5.3 Full objects.

```
STACK: type module is
   const
      MAX_STACK_SIZE = 100;

   procedure PUSH (S: STACK; ITEM: integer);
   procedure POP  (S: STACK; ITEM: integer);
end;

STACK: type module body is
   type STACK is
      record
         CONTENTS: array [1..MAX_STACK_SIZE] of integer;
         SIZE: integer;
      end;

   procedure PUSH (S: STACK; ITEM: integer) is
   begin
      if (S.SIZE < MAX_STACK_SIZE) then
         S.SIZE := S.SIZE + 1;
         S.CONTENTS[S.SIZE] := ITEM;
      else
         -- Handle full stack error
      end if;
   end;

   procedure POP (S: STACK; ITEM: integer) is
   begin
      if (S.SIZE /= 0) then
         ITEM := S.CONTENTS[S.SIZE];
         S.SIZE := S.SIZE - 1;
      else
         --  Handle empty stack error
      end if;
   end;
begin
   STACK.SIZE := 0;
end;
```

Figure 5.4 Use of state and initialization.

```
STACK: type module is
   const
      MAX_STACK_SIZE = 100;

   procedure PUSH (ITEM: integer);
   procedure POP  (ITEM: integer);
end;


STACK: type module body is
   type
      STACK is array [1..MAX_STACK_SIZE] of integer;
   var
      S: STACK
      SIZE: integer;

   procedure PUSH (ITEM: integer) is
   begin
      if (SIZE < MAX_STACK_SIZE) then
         SIZE := SIZE + 1;
         S[SIZE] := ITEM;
      else
         -- Handle full stack error
      end if;
   end;

   procedure POP (ITEM: integer) is
   begin
      if (SIZE /= 0) then
         ITEM := S[SIZE];
         SIZE := SIZE - 1;
      else
         --  Handle empty stack error
      end if;
   end;

begin
   SIZE := 0;
end;
```

Figure 5.5 Information hiding.

into the variable NEW_ITEM. The method part

    POP(NEW_ITEM)

is considered as a "message" that is "sent" to object S1.

5.3 ABSTRACT DATA TYPES

A major decision during program design concerns the representation of data. For example, a stack could be represented either by an array or by a linked list of elements. In languages like Fortran or standard Pascal, the results of the decision are likely to permeate the entire program because the representation is essentially public knowledge. Even though standard Pascal makes a beginning to a type definition, it is still obvious how a new type is represented. Although we might have the type definition

```
type STACK = record
             SIZE: integer;
             CONTENTS: array[1..100] of integer;
         end;
```

a stack can still be accessed directly through subscripted references to the field CONTENTS.

In contrast to this, a program written in Mini-language Objects, which has similar facilities, will operate on the stack through operations provided by the type module. The user is forced to use only the user-defined operations, for example, PUSH and POP, because the representation of the type is unavailable.

The hiding of the representation is consistent with the use of primitive types in a language. The definition of a language gives no clue as to the internal representation of the primitive objects. Integers might be represented as two's complement binary numbers or binary-coded decimal digits. In most languages, there is no way of finding out the particular representation without investigating the implementation.

What characterizes the primitive types is the set of operations that manipulate them. A type that is defined entirely by a set of operations is called an *abstract data type*. The operations provide a representation-independent specification. A language that supports abstract data types is one that allows the user to define new abstract types beyond the primitive ones. In Mini-language Objects, the specification of a data type is entirely in the operation-description part of the type module. The examples of Figures

4.4 and 4.5 define abstract data types, as do the four examples of Figure 5.3.

In short, there are two major advantages to defining a type as an abstract data type:

1. The separation of operations from questions of representation results in data independence. The representation can be changed without corresponding changes in the main part of the program, and the correctness of the program will be unaffected.

2. The operations can be itemized in a list and made clear to the user.

5.4 TURBO PASCAL

Turbo Pascal (see Borland 1989) embeds an object-oriented approach in the framework of standard Pascal. Turbo Pascal objects are like standard Pascal record types enhanced with the ability to include procedures and functions as second components. The procedures and functions become the "member functions."

Figure 5.6 shows an example of two Turbo Pascal objects. The Turbo Pascal approach mirrors quite closely the idea that a type is a set of objects and operations. The example of Figure 5.6 is drawn from [Borland 1989] and will be discussed again in Chapter 7 on Inheritance.

FURTHER READING

Abstract data types are really a fundamental idea in the theory of programming languages and in programming. The book by [Cleaveland 86] presents a good treatment of types in general.

The basic idea for object-oriented programming is present in the concept of a class in Simula 67. Following this pioneering work, there was a sequence of experimental languages — Clu, Mesa, Alphard, Euclid, and Gipsy.

Abstract data types were first introduced in [Liskov and Zilles 1974]. The method of formal specification was first introduced in [Guttag 1977].

An excellent discussion of the object-oriented approach is given in [Booch 1991].

```
unit POINTS;
interface
   uses GRAPH;
   type
     LOCATION = object
         X, Y: integer;
         procedure INIT: (NEWX, NEWY: integer);
         function XCOORD: integer;
         function YCOORD: integer;
     end;
     POINT = object(LOCATION)
         VISIBLE: boolean;
         procedure INIT (NEWX, NEWY: integer);
         procedure MOVE_TO (NEWX, NEWY: integer);
         procedure HIDE;
         procedure SHOW;
         function IS_VISIBLE: boolean;
     end;
end;


implementation
   procedure LOCATION.INIT (NEWX, NEWY: integer);
   begin
     X := NEWX;
     Y := NEWY;
   end;

   function LOCATION.XCOORD: integer;
   begin
     XCOORD := X;
   end;

   function LOCATION.YCOORD: integer;
   begin
     YCOORD := Y;
   end;
```

Figure 5.6   Objects in Turbo Pascal.

```
procedure POINT.INIT (NEWX, NEWY: integer);
begin
   LOCATION.INIT (NEWX, NEWY);
   VISIBLE := false;
end;

procedure POINT.MOVE_TO (NEWX, NEWY);
begin
   HIDE;
   X := NEWX;
   Y := NEWY;
   SHOW;
end;

procedure POINT.HIDE;
begin
   VISIBLE := false;
   REMOVE_PIXEL (X, Y);
end;

procedure POINT.SHOW;
begin
   VISIBLE := true;
   DRAW.PUT_PIXEL (X, Y);
end;

function POINT.IS_VISIBLE: boolean;
begin
   return VISIBLE;
end;

end;
```

Figure 5.6 (continued)

EXERCISES

Exercise 5.1 *Multiple Choice*

Pick the answer that best fits the question.

1. In Mini-language Objects,
   a. a main program contains no type declarations.
   b. the visible part of a type module contains no parameter names.
   c. an operation can return a value.
   d. all of the above.
   e. two of the above.

2. An abstract data type is
   a. a way of defining new types.
   b. a type whose representation is hidden.
   c. a set of objects and the operations on the objects.
   d. essentially a synonym for a user-defined type.
   e. all of the above; there is no common definition.

3. In the STACK example of Figure 5.2,
   a. many stacks can be declared.
   b. PUSH will only work on one stack.
   c. the maximum stack size can be changed.
   d. the type of stack element is specified when a stack variable is declared.
   e. the type STACK is visible to the user of the type module.

4. Which of the following is not a programming-language construct:
   a. Type constructor.
   b. Instance variable.
   c. Operator definition.
   d. Module.
   e. Dynamic binding.

5. Consider the following declarations (from Borland 's Turbo Pascal 5.5):

```
type
    ITEM = object
        NAME: string[10];
        procedure print;
    end;
var
    M: ITEM;
```

The variable M is called
a.   an instance.
b.   an object.
c.   an object type.
d.   a message.
e.   a global variable.

6.   In the previous example, ITEM is called
a.   an instance.
b.   an object.
c.   an object type.
d.   a message.
e.   a private type.

7.   Which of the following is not really a true statement from an object-oriented perspective?
a.   A record type is a composite type.
b.   Information hiding applies to type declarations.
c.   Classes define types.
d.   July 4, 1994, is an object.
e.   A class must be separately compiled.

Exercise 5.2 *Information Hiding*

The actual representation of the values of a data type is in the implementation part of a type module of Mini-language Objects. It is intended that the compiler should not require access to this information while compiling other type modules or the main part of the program. This ensures that the programmer of other parts of the program cannot make use of this private information. Is this possible or must the representation be made available to the compiler? What are the advantages and disadvantages of doing this?

Exercise 5.3 *An Abstract Data Type*

The following is a specification for the abstract data type BAG:

```
BAG:  type module
   EMPTY_BAG:  ()  => BAG;
   INSERT:     (BAG, integer) => BAG;
   DELETE:     (BAG, integer) => BAG;
   IS_MEMBER:  (BAG, integer) => boolean;

B: BAG;
```

```
    INT_A, INT_B: integer;

Axioms
    IS_MEMBER(EMPTY_BAG(), INT_A) = false;
    IS_MEMBER(INSERT(B, INT_A), INT_B) =
        if (INT_A = INT_B)
            true
        else
            IS_MEMBER(B, INT_B)

    DELETE(EMPTY_BAG(), INT_A) = EMPTY_BAG()
    DELETE(INSERT(B, INT_A), INT_B) =
        if (INT_A = INT_B)
            B
        else
            INSERT(DELETE(B,  INT_B), INT_A)
```

Provide an implementation part for the BAG type module in Mini-language Modules extended to include arrays as an additional data structure.

Exercise 5.4 *The SET Abstract Data Type*

Construct a specification for the abstract type SET that corresponds to the mathematical concept of a set. This specification will differ in a small, but important, detail from the specification of the BAG data type in Exercise 5.3. Explain the reason for the difference.

CHAPTER 6

Classes

"The programming paradigm is: Decide which classes you want; provide a full set of operations for each class; make commonality explicit by using inheritance."

[Bjarne Stroustrup 1988]

"Class design is type design."

[Scott Meyers 1992]

Stroustrup

[Stroustrup 1988] makes a distinction between "enabling" a program style and "supporting" a program style. A programming language enables a program style if it is possible, with discipline and effort, to achieve the style. A programming language supports a program style if it makes it convenient to achieve the style.

Mini-language Classes contains a number of small differences from the previous mini-language. These differences support object-oriented programming in various ways and are a somewhat natural consequence of using modules that define a class of objects.

These terms are especially relevant to this chapter:

Abstract Data Type	A type whose representation is not available to the user.
Class	A programming language construct similar to a module. The module itself is the type.

Instance	An object, i.e., a member of a class.
Instance Variable	A variable that is defined within a module defining a class. The variable is part of the internal state of the object.
Constructor	A procedure that initializes an object, e.g., by allocating storage or setting a local state.
Destructor	A procedure that cleans up after an object is no longer used.

6.1   MINI-LANGUAGE CLASSES

Figure 6.1 defines the syntax of Mini-Language Classes. This mini-language is similar to the previous mini-language. In Mini-language Classes, the phrase "type module" has been replaced by the word "class." This is in line with the now familiar term used in object-oriented programming. A class is a programming language construct defining a type. User-defined types are thus considered to be classes. In Mini-language Classes, the predefined types integer, boolean, and string are also considered to be classes.

A program in Mini-language Classes consists of a main part (containing variable declarations and executable statements) and a set of *classes*. Each class implements a single, user-defined data type used in the main part. If the main part uses only primitive types, no classes are given.

In both the main part and the classes, the usual assignment, loop, if, input, and output statements can all be used. A declaration in the main part defines a list of variables to be either one of the primitive types or of some type that is defined by a class of the same name. Consider, for example, the following declaration section:

```
TODAY, TOMORROW: DATE;
DAY_NUMBER, MONTH_NUMBER, YEAR_NUMBER: integer;
```

Here the type DATE must be defined by a class named DATE. There must be a class describing each (nonprimitive) type being used. The classes and the main part are compiled separately and linked together before execution.

Classes

A class consists of two parts: a visible part and an implementation part. The visible part defines operations for the type. The operations can make use of

Figure 6.1   Mini-language Classes.

```
program                ::=  main-part
                       [    class ]...

main-part              ::=  program
                                variable-declaration...
                            begin
                                statement...
                            end ;
type-module            ::=  identifier : class
                                operation-description...
                            implementation
                                variable-declaration...
                                operation-algorithm...
                            end ;
variable-declaration   ::=  identifier [ , identifier ]... : type ;
type                   ::=  integer | boolean | string | identifier
operation-description  ::=  designator : ([ type [ , type ]... ])
                                                [ => type ] ;
designator             ::=  identifier | operator
operation-algorithm    ::=  operation : designator ([ identifier
                                                [ , identifier ]... ) is
                                variable-declaration...
                            begin
                                statement...
                            [ return expression ; ]
                            end ;
statement              ::=  assignment-statement | call-statement
                       |    if-statement |      loop-statement | input-statement
                       |    output-statement
assignment-statement   ::=  variable := expression ;
call-statement         ::=  call ;
if-statement           ::=  if ( expression )
                                if-option
                       [    else
                                if-option
if-option              ::=  statement | { statement... }
loop-statement         ::=  while expression loop
                                statement...
                            end loop ;
```

Figure 6.1 (continued)

input-statement	::= **input** variable [, variable]... ;
output-statement	::= **output** expression [, expression]... ;
expression	::= operand [operator operand]
operand	::= integer | boolean | string | variable | call
	| (expression)
call	::= simple-call | identifier . simple-call
simple-call	::= identifier (expression [, expression]...)
variable	::= identifier
operator	::= < | = | ≠ | > | + | - | * | **div** | **and** |**or**

types defined by other classes in the program. The operations can manipulate values of the type being defined and perform conversions between these values and values of other types. The implementation part must contain the statements that perform the operations defined in the interface specification.

The visible part of the class DATE might, for example, consist of the following descriptions:

```
DATE: class
    SET_DATE:    (integer, integer, integer) => DATE;
    DATE_YEAR:   (DATE) => integer;
    DATE_MONTH:  (DATE) => integer;
    DATE_DAY:    (DATE) => integer;
    +:           (DATE, integer) => DATE;
end;
```

This module is similar to the type module DATE in the previous chapter.

The implementation part of a module provides the details required to make the complete program workable. It includes variable and type declarations describing internal values, and the actual algorithms for the operations defined in the interface specification. The operation algorithms have the same form as in Mini-language Objects. The types of local variables can be defined by other classes.

A major element in Mini-language Classes is the way the objects of a class are represented. For example, consider the class COMPLEX introduced in the previous chapter. In Mini-language Objects, a record type declaration is given for the type COMPLEX in the implementation part of the module for the class. For example, we have

```
type COMPLEX =
   record
      REAL: integer;
      IMAG: integer;
   end;
```

In Mini-language Classes, this situation is handled differently. Two variables represent the real and imaginary parts of a complex number. These variables are given in the implementation part of the module for the class. In particular, we have

```
REAL: integer;
IMAG: integer;
```

Thus, rather than a representation of the type, the storage required for objects of a given class is given through a series of variables in the implementation part of the module for the class. These variables are called *instance variables.* Because these variables will have a value once an object is used in a program or procedure, we speak of the "state" of an object.

An implementation part may contain one or more *constructors*. In Mini-language Classes a constructor is an operation whose name is the same as the class. A constructor is a special procedure that is invoked when an object is *declared.* If more than one constructor is given, the constructors must differ from each other by the number or type of their parameters, i.e., the overloading must be valid.

A feature of Mini-language Classes is the way a method can be invoked. Consider the conventional call

```
REAL_PART(Z)
```

This is a call to a function; the call returns the real part of Z. Consider the equivalent call of Mini-language Classes:

```
Z.REAL_PART()
```

This is the dot notation, a common object-oriented notation mentioned in the previous chapter. The method part

```
REAL_PART()
```

is considered as a "message," which is "sent" to the object z.

The remainder of Mini-language Classes is in the style of the previous mini-languages.

Example

Figure 6.2 shows the complex number example introduced in the previous chapters redone using Mini-language Classes. It performs operations on complex numbers and makes use of symbols, such as + and =, to overload operators, as is done in Mini-languge Modules and Mini-language Typedef. Here the type COMPLEX is the name of the class. The representation of the type is defined in the implementation part of the class by the two variables REAL and IMAG.

As mentioned in the previous chapter, an alternative COMPLEX class might have an internal representation of the values using polar coordinates. To do this would probably require a new type, ANGLE, and a set of operations including the trigonometric functions. These could be provided in a separate class. Here, however, these changes could be made *without* altering the interface specification for COMPLEX. Thus, any program that uses the type COMPLEX would not need to be changed.

Consider next the following main program:

```
program
    X,Y,Z: COMPLEX;
begin
    X.SET_COMPLEX(1, 1);
    Y.SET_COMPLEX(2, 2);
    Z := X + Y;
    output Z.REAL(), Z.IMAG();
end;
```

This program prints

```
3    3
```

Now consider this

```
program
    X:   COMPLEX(1,1);
    Y:   COMPLEX(2,2);
    Z:   COMPLEX;
begin
    Z := X + Y;
    output Z.REAL(), Z.IMAG();
end;
```

This program also prints

```
3    3
```

```
program
   X, Y, Z: COMPLEX;
   R_VAL, I_VAL: integer;
begin
   input R_VAL, I_VAL;
   X.SET_CPLX(R_VAL, I_VAL);
   input R_VAL, I_VAL;
   Y.SET_CPLX(R_VAL, I_VAL);
   if (X = Y)
      Z := X + Y;
   else
      Z := X - Y;
   R_VAL := Z.REAL( );
   I_VAL := Z.IMAG( );
   output R_VAL, I_VAL;
end;

COMPLEX: class
   COMPLEX:    (integer);
   COMPLEX:    (integer, integer);
   SET_CPLX:   (integer, integer);
   =:          (COMPLEX, COMPLEX) => boolean;
   +:          (COMPLEX, COMPLEX) => COMPLEX;
   -:          (COMPLEX, COMPLEX) => COMPLEX;
   REAL_PART: ( ) => integer;
   IMAG_PART: ( ) => integer;

implementation
   REAL: integer;
   IMAG: integer;

   operation: COMPLEX (VALUE) is
   begin
      REAL := VALUE;   IMAG := 0;
   end;

   operation: COMPLEX (VALUE1, VALUE2) is
   begin
      REAL := VALUE1;   IMAG := VALUE2;
   end;
```

Figure 6.2   Mini-language Classes program.

```
    operation: SET_CPLX (R_PART, I_PART) is
    begin
       REAL := R_PART;   IMAG := I_PART;
    end;

    operation : = (A, B) is
       RESULT: boolean;
    begin
       if (A.REAL = B.REAL)
          if (A.IMAG = B.IMAG)
             RESULT := true;
          else
             RESULT := false;
       else
          RESULT := false;
       return RESULT;
    end;

    operation : + (A, B) is
       RESULT: COMPLEX;
    begin
       RESULT.REAL := A.REAL + B.REAL;
       RESULT.IMAG := A.IMAG + B.IMAG;
       return RESULT;
    end;

    operation : * (A, B) is
       RESULT: COMPLEX;
    begin
       RESULT.REAL := A.REAL*B.REAL - A.IMAG*B.IMAG;
       RESULT.IMAG := A.REAL*B.IMAG + A.IMAG*B.REAL;
       return RESULT;
    end;

    operation: REAL_PART ( ) is begin
       return REAL;
    end;

    operation: IMAG_PART ( ) is begin
       return IMAG;
    end;
end;
```

Figure 6.2   (continued)

This program makes use of a constructor.

Consider next the main program:

```
program
    X: COMPLEX(1);
    Y: COMPLEX(2,2);
    Z: COMPLEX;
begin
    Z := X + Y;
    output Z.REAL(), Z.IMAG()
end;
```

This program prints

3   2

In this example two different constructors are called. One constructor has one argument; the other has two arguments.

6.2 MORE ON OBJECTS

We return again to our stack example given in the previous chapters.

Consider Figure 6.3, which falls in line with the sequence of stack examples in Chapter 5. In this version also, STACK is the name of the class, reflecting the point that the entire purpose of the class is to define a single type. Given the definitions of Figure 6.3, a programmer could write a program declaring different stack objects; for example, one might see declarations like

```
S1, S2: STACK;
```

Here the programmer would introduce two stack structures called S1 and S2. They could be manipulated using the procedures PUSH and POP given in the class. They are automatically initialized in that SIZE is set to 0.

Figure 6.3 also makes use of information hiding, which is required in Mini-language Classes. Stack variables do not appear in the parameter lists. Stack s is part of the state of the object. s becomes an *instance variable*.

To work with stacks, the dot notation is used. For example, we may see a statement like

```
S1.PUSH(6);
```

This statement pushes the value 6 onto stack S1.

In the previous examples, the maximum stack size was established as a constant in the visible part of the package. The initial size, 0, was set in a kind of "initialization" part of the package. In Figure 6.4 a different approach is taken.

The stack example of Figure 6.4 contains two constructors: (a) one with no parameters, which sets the initial size to 0, and (b) one with one parameter, which establishes the maximum stack size and sets the initial size to 0. Thus, we may have

```
S1: STACK;          -- invokes the first constructor

S2: STACK(500);     -- invokes the second constructor
```

A parameter-less constructor is essentially a default constructor..

The use of such procedures is common in object-oriented programming. Such procedures have a name. In C++, they are called *constructors*. In Eiffel, they are called *creation procedures*.

6.3 SMALLTALK AND EIFFEL

Smalltalk

The language Smalltalk is one of the pioneering works in object-oriented programming. Its data abstraction ideas are cast in a somewhat different form from languages like Modula 2 and Ada.

Computation in Smalltalk consists of sending *messages* to *objects*. An object consists of some memory and a set of operations. Objects may represent numbers, queues, dictionaries, programs, or other kinds of data. The nature of an object's operations depends on the kind of thing it represents. An object that represents a number would have operations that compute arithmetic functions.

A message is a request for an object to perform one of its functions. The message specifies the operation to be performed but not how the operation should be carried out. It is up to the receiver of the message to determine how the operation is to be performed. The set of messages to which an object can respond is its *interface*. In a similar way to the types in Mini-language Classes, the only way in which an object can be manipulated is through its interface. The private memory of an object can only be manipulated by its operations. Thus, we have data abstraction through objects.

```
STACK: class is
   const MAX_STACK_SIZE = 100;

   procedure PUSH (ITEM: integer);
   procedure POP  (ITEM: integer);
end;

STACK: class body is
   type
      STACK is array [1..MAX_STACK_SIZE] of integer;
   var
      S: STACK;
      SIZE: integer;

   procedure PUSH (ITEM: integer) is
   begin
      if (SIZE < MAX_STACK_SIZE) then
         SIZE := SIZE + 1;
         S[SIZE] := ITEM;
      else
         -- Handle full stack error
      end if;
   end;

   procedure POP (ITEM: integer) is
   begin
      if (SIZE /= 0) then
         ITEM := S[SIZE];
         SIZE := SIZE - 1;
      else
         --  Handle empty stack error
      end if;
   end;
begin
   SIZE := 0;
end;
```

Figure 6.3   Full objects (information hiding).

```
STACK: class is
   procedure PUSH (ITEM: integer);
   procedure POP  (ITEM: integer);
end;

STACK: class body is
   type STACK is array [1..MAX_STACK_SIZE] of integer;
   var
     S: STACK;
     SIZE: integer;
     MAX_STACK_SIZE: integer;

   constructor STACK () is begin
     SIZE := 0;
     MAX_STACK_SIZE := 100;
   end;

   constructor STACK (V: integer) is begin
     SIZE := 0;
     MAX_STACK_SIZE := V;
   end;

   procedure PUSH (ITEM: integer) is
   begin
     if (SIZE < MAX_STACK_SIZE) then
        SIZE := SIZE + 1;
        S[SIZE] := ITEM;
     else
        -- Handle full stack error
     end if;
   end;

   procedure POP (ITEM: integer) is
   begin
     if (SIZE /= 0) then
        ITEM := S[SIZE];
        SIZE := SIZE - 1;
     else
        --  Handle empty stack error
     end if;
   end;
end;
```

Figure 6.4 Constructors.

Each object is an instance of a *class*. All objects of the same class have identical message interfaces. Each class has a name so that it can be referenced. A class also has a protocol description that lists the messages that can be understood by objects of the class and an implementation description that defines how the operations of the class are implemented.

An example of a class is Financial History. Objects of this class have operations available through its interface. These operations are as follows:

1. Create a new object of the class with an initial amount of money.

2. Note that a certain amount of money was spent for a certain reason.

3. Note that a certain amount of money was received from a particular source.

4. Find out how much money is available.

5. Find out how much money has been spent for a particular reason.

6. Find out how much money has been received from a particular source.

The protocol description would list these operations, showing what the parameters are. For example:

```
receive: amount from: source     Remember that amount has been
                                  received from source.
```

The implementation description would list the names of variables that belong to each object and the way in which the operations are performed. Thus, part of the implementation description for Financial History might be

```
class name:              Financial History
instance variable names: cashOnHand
                         incomes
                         expenditures
instance methods:
transaction recording
   receive: amount from: source
      incomes at: source
         put (self totalReceivedFrom: source) + amount
      cashOnHand <- cashOnHand + amount
```

The instance variable names are the names of variables individually part of each instance of an object of the class.

The major difference between the class concept of Smalltalk and data abstraction as we have described elsewhere in this chapter is that the variables are typeless; they are thus more flexible than classes.

Eiffel

Eiffel [Meyers 1992] is a special language for object-oriented programming. It was designed specifically around the object-oriented paradigm. In particular:

(a) It is a language in the Algol, Pascal, Modula, and Ada tradition.

(b) It has a thorough implementation of object-oriented concepts.

(c) It is a rather bold approach in the choice of its concepts and its exclusion of certain concepts (e.g., enumeration types, subrange types, exits, and global variables) often considered essential.

The following is a sketch of a simple class in Eiffel:

```
class interface PHONE_ENTRY
     feature
         LAST_NAME:   STRING;
         FIRST_NAME:  STRING;
         PHONE_NUM:   STRING;
         PRINT () is
              do
                 ...
              end;
     end;
```

Among the features of Eiffel are the following:

(a) Numerous features to support object-oriented design and programming.

(b) The ability to define precise, low-level semantics for object creation, copying, and assignment.

(c) The use of assertions and invariants to guarantee behavior.

(d) Generic class parameters.

(e) A mechanism for exception handling.

FURTHER READING

Smalltalk and Simula 67 are pioneering works in object-oriented programming.
The following works offer good discussions of support for the OOP paradigm: [Stroustrup 1988], making objects that have the full support as built-in types; [Ada Rationale 1995], an approach to full OOP using packages as a basis; [Meyers 1992], which motivates support issues and innovative solutions in OOP.

EXERCISES

Exercise 6.1 *Multiple Choice*

Pick the answer that best fits the question.

1. In Mini-language Classes,
    a. a main program contains no type declarations.
    b. a class contains no type declarations.
    c. a constructor can have no parameters.
    d. all of the above.
    e. two of the above.

2. Which of the following is not a programming language construct in Mini-language Classes:
    a. Derived type.
    b. Instance variable.
    c. Operator definition.
    d. Module.
    e. Member function.

3. Which of the following distinguishes Mini-language Classes from Mini-language Objects?
    a. In Mini-language Classes an operation can have a result type.
    b. In Mini-language Classes, the visible part of a module only allows the declaration of operations.
    c. In Mini-language Classes, strings are allowed.
    d. In Mini-language Objects, arrays are allowed.
    e. In Mini-language Objects, record types are allowed.

4. A constructor is called
    a. when a program is started.
    b. when a type is defined.
    c. when a variable is declared.

d.   when a class is initialized.
e.   when a block is entered.

5.   In OOP, a "message" is like a
a.   procedure call.
b.   string.
c.   record structure.
d.   Pascal variable.
e.   file.

6.   Which of the following is unlikely to be found in a class?
a.   A procedure declaration.
b.   A type declaration.
c.   An exception handler.
d.   A task.
e.   None of the above, they are all possible.

7.   Which of the following is not really a true statement from an object-oriented perspective?
a.   Messages are sent to objects.
b.   The representation of an abstract data type is not visible to a user of the types.
c.   The state of an object is defined by its instance variables.
d.   Language mechanisms are important in OOP.
e.   Algorithms are important in OOP.

Exercise 6.2 *Floating Point Arithmetic*

Design a class for the data type FLOAT that would allow the language to be extended to include floating point arithmetic.

Exercise 6.3 *String Handling*

With good design, one can write a public interface for handling strings. Write the visible part of a class for a type STRING. Use a syntax similar to Mini-language Classes. You may ignore the built-in type string in Mini-language Classes. The design should consider the following operations:

Concatenate two strings to form a new string.
Extract a portion of a string.
Search within a string for a given substring.
Obtain the length of a string.
Delete a substring or replace it by another substring, not necessarily of the same length.
Insert a string within another string at a specified point.

Note: In Chapter 2, we described how character strings can either be viewed as a primitive type of the language, as in Mini-language Type, or treated as vectors of the primitive type character.

Exercise 6.4 *Separate Compilation of Classes*

Three basic issues in separate compilation of languages with classes are
  (1) separate compilation of a class itself
  (2) separating the visible part of a class from the implementation part and allowing separate compilation of each part
  (3) syntax

Write a short (two or three page) report on these or other pertinent issues.

CHAPTER 7

Inheritance

> *The problem is there is no distinction between the general properties of any shape (a shape has a color, it can be drawn, etc.) and the properties of a specific shape (a circle is a shape that has a radius, is drawn by a circle-drawing function, etc.). The ability to express this distinction and take advantage of it defines object-oriented programming.*
>
> [Stroustrup 1988]

> *The key idea of programming by extension is the ability to declare a new type that refines an existing type by inheriting, modifying or adding to both the existing components and the operations of the parent type.*
>
> [Ada Rationale 1995]

In the popular literature on software, the phrase "software reuse" is familiar. Inheritance is the means by which object-oriented programming achieves software reuse. With inheritance, new classes can be derived using previously defined classes as building blocks

"Inheritance" is really not the best word for the phenomenon it represents. When we think of the word inheritance in everyday usage, we often think of something akin to a parent–child relationship or, say, the relation implied by siblings or cousins. There are natural corollaries to the sibling or cousin relation implied by inheritance. The idea of a class called "shape" with subclasses of polygon, rectangle, and circle follows quite naturally. Likewise, the idea of an account as a class with subclasses of checking account and savings account also follows in this light.

The word "inheritance," however, implies even more. It means deriving one type from another type and making use of any of the previously defined properties, even if the two types are not "descendants." In [Ada Rationale, 1995], the phrase "Programming by Extension" is used. Thus, it makes sense to derive the types point and circle from the type location. Perhaps the phrase "derived type" or "extended type" might be better than the word "inheritance."

We introduce these terms in this chapter:

Constructor	A procedure that initializes an object, e.g., by allocating storage or setting a local state.
Destructor	A procedure that cleans up after an object is no longer used.
Inheritance	Deriving a new type or class from an existing type or class.
Multiple Inheritance	Deriving a type from more than one parent type.
Polymorphism	Use of the same name for an operation whose meaning depends upon the types of its arguments.

7.1   MINI-LANGUAGE INHERIT

Figure 7.1 defines the syntax of Mini-language Inherit. This mini-language is very similar to the previous mini-language. In Mini-language Inherit, the phrase "type module" has been replaced by the word "class." This is in line with the now familiar term used in object-oriented programming. A class is a programming-language construct defining a type. User-defined types are thus considered to be classes. In Mini-language Inherit, the predefined types integer, boolean, and string are also considered to be classes.

The major change in Mini-language Inherit is the use of inheritance. A class can be derived from another class. Consider the line

```
class B derived (A);
```

Here the class B is derived from the class A. This means that the operations

Figure 7.1   Mini-language Inherit.

program	::= main-part
	[class-module]...
main-part	::= **program**
	variable-declaration...
	begin
	statement...
	end ;
class-module	::= identifier : **class** [**derived** (identifier)]
	variable-declaration ...
	operation-description ...
	implementation
	variable-declaration...
	operation-algorithm...
	end ;
variable-declaration	::= identifier [**,** identifier]... **:** class-name **;**
operation-description	::= designator : (**[** class-name
	[, class-name]...]) [**=>** class-name] **;**
class-name	::= identifier | **integer** | **boolean** | **string**
designator	::= identifier | operator
operation-algorithm	::= designator : **operation** ([identifier
	[**,** identifier]...]) **is**
	variable-declaration...
	begin
	statement...
	[**return** expression **;**]
	end ;
statement	::= assignment-statement | call-statement | if-statement
	| loop-statement | input-statement | output-statement
assignment-statement	::= variable **:=** expression **;**
call-statement	::= **call ;**
if-statement	::= **if** (expression)
	if-option
	[**else**
	if-option]
if-option	::= statement | { statement... }
loop-statement	::= **while** expression **loop**
	statement...
	end loop ;
input-statement	::= **input** variable [**,** variable]... **;**
output-statement	::= **output** expression [**,** expression]... **;**

Figure 7.1   (continued)

```
expression        ::= operand [ operator operand ]
operand           ::= integer | boolean | string | variable | call
                  | ( expression )
call              ::= simple-call | identifier . simple-call
simple-call       ::= identifier ( [ expression [ , expression]... ] )
variable          ::= identifier | variable . identifier
operator          ::= < | = | ≠ | > | + | - | * | div | and | or
```

---

defined for the class A also apply to the class B. It also means that the instance variables for the class A are considered as instance variables for the class B.

An operation in a class may be redefined in a derived class. The new definition overrides the previous definition. Notice that for redefinition of an operation, the number of arguments and the types of arguments are the same in each class. Otherwise the new definition would be an overloading.

Note that (see the program by Klenz in [Survey 1993])

```
DATE: class
    YEAR: integer
    MONTH: integer
    DAY: integer
end
```

is a perfectly valid class in Mini-language Inherit. This is the same as a record type definition in previous mini-languages. Thus, we may have

```
D: DATE;
...
D.YEAR := D.YEAR + 1;
```

7.2   INHERITANCE

As mentioned at the beginning of this chapter, "inheritance" may not be the best word. Ada 9.X uses the phrase "programming by extension." This is an apt phrase and better conveys the spirit of inheritance.

Suppose that we have a defined type or class whose behavior is not quite appropriate for the application we have in mind. With inheritance, we can take the existing class and create a derived class. In the derived class,

```
class STUDENT
   SOC_SOC_NUM: integer;
   YEAR: integer;
   procedure GET_STUDENT_INFO;
implementation
   procedure GET_STUDENT_INFO is begin
      output "Enter Social Security Number: ";
      input SOC_SEC_NUM;
      output "Enter grade level: ";
      input YEAR;
   end;
end;

class HIGH_SCHOOL_STUDENT derived (STUDENT);
   procedure PRINT_STUDENT_INFO;
implementation
   procedure PRINT_STUDENT_ INFO is begin
      output "Social security number is ", SOC_SEC_NUM;
      if      (YEAR =  9) output "Student is a freshman";
      else if (YEAR = 10) output "Student is a sophomore";
      else if (YEAR = 11) output "Student is a junior";
      else if (YEAR = 12) output "Student is a senior";
   end;
end;

class COLLEGE_STUDENT derived (STUDENT);
   MAJOR: string;
   procedure GET_MAJOR;
   procedure PRINT_STUDENT_INFO;
implementation
   procedure GET_MAJOR is begin
      output "Enter major";
      input MAJOR;
   end;
   procedure PRINT_STUDENT_INFO is begin
     output "Social security number is ", SOC_SEC_NUM;
     output "Student's major is ", MAJOR;
     if      (YEAR = 13) output "Student is a college freshman";
     else if(YEAR = 14) output "Student is a college sophomore";
     else if(YEAR = 15) output "Student is a college junior";
     else if(YEAR = 16) output "Student is a college senior";
   end;
end;
```

Figure 7.2   A simple example of inheritance.

```
LOCATION: class
   INIT:   (NEWX, NEWY: integer);
   XCOORD: ( ) => integer;
   YCOORD: ( ) => integer;

implementation
   X: integer;
   Y: integer;

   INIT: (NEWX, NEWY: integer) is begin
      X := NEWX;
      Y := NEWY;
   end;

   XCOORD: ( ) => integer is begin
      XCOORD := X;
   end;

   YCOORD: ( ) => integer is begin
      YCOORD := Y;
   end;
end;


POINT: class derived(LOCATION)
   INIT:       (NEWX, NEWY: integer);
   MOVE_TO:    (NEWX, NEWY: integer);
   HIDE:       ( );
   SHOW:       ( );
   IS_VISIBLE:( ) => boolean;

implementation
   VISIBLE: integer;

   INIT: (NEWX, NEWY: integer) is begin
      LOCATION.INIT (NEWX, NEWY);
      VISIBLE := false;
   end;
```

Figure 7.3 Use of inheritance.

```
   SHOW ( ) is begin
      VISIBLE := true;
      DRAW.PUT_PIXEL (X, Y);
   end;

   HIDE ( ) is begin
      VISIBLE := false;
      REMOVE_PIXEL (X, Y);
   end;

   function IS_VISIBLE ( ) => boolean is begin
      return VISIBLE;
   end;

   procedure MOVE_TO (NEWX, NEWY) is begin
      HIDE;
      X := NEWX;
      Y := NEWY;
      SHOW;
   end;
end;

CIRCLE: class derived (POINT)
   INIT:        (INITX, INITY, INIT_RADIUS: integer);
   MOVE_TO:     (NEWX, NEWY: integer);
   HIDE:        ( );
   SHOW:        ( );
   EXPAND:      (INCREMENT: integer);
   CONTRACT:    (DECREMENT: integer);

implementation
   RADIUS: integer;

   INIT: operation (INITX, INITY, INITRADIUS: integer) is
   begin
      POINT.INIT (INITX, INITY);
      RADIUS := INITRADIUS;
   end;
   SHOW: operation ( ) is begin
      VISIBLE := true;
      DRAW.MAKE_CIRCLE (X, Y, RADIUS);
   end;
```

Figure 7.3   (continued)

```
HIDE: operation ( ) is begin
   VISIBLE := false;
   DRAW.REMOVE_CIRCLE (X, Y, RADIUS);
end;

EXPAND: operation (INCREMENT: integer) is
begin
   HIDE;
   RADIUS := RADIUS + INCREMENT;
   SHOW;
end;

CONTRACT: operation (DECREMENT: integer) is
begin
   HIDE;
   RADIUS := RADIUS - DECREMENT;
   SHOW;
end;

operation MOVE_TO: (NEWX, NEWY, INITRADIUS: integer) is
begin
   HIDE;
   X := NEWX;
   Y := NEWY;
   SHOW;
end;
end;
```

Figure 7.3   (continued)

we will add a new procedure as one of the operations. This procedure will reflect the new behavior. The effort and creativity in the original type or class will still remain and still be usable.

Now let us suppose we have a defined type or class and want to modify the definition with additional information. This again brings in inheritance. We can define a new class, a derived class, with an additional field or instance variable kept as part of the new class. We will, of course, need to add procedures of functions that make use of this new field, but, again, we can keep the other effort and creativity devised for the original class.

A simple yet effective use of inheritance is shown in Figure 7.2. This example is based on an example due to [Croy 1993]. Here we have a simple class called STUDENT with two instance variables and one operation, a procedure called GET_STUDENT_INFO. Two classes are derived from this class, one called HIGH_SCHOOL_STUDENT and the other called COLLEGE_STUDENT. Both of these classes add a procedure to the base class. This procedure is PRINT_STUDENT_INFO. The class COLLEGE_STUDENT also adds a data field, MAJOR, and a procedure, GET_MAJOR.

These two derived classes are certainly elementary. Both contain a procedure with slightly different effects on output; one of the derived classes adds additional meaning. We might view the two derived classes as simple extensions of the original class. Given the base class STUDENT, we add a little semantics to this class in order to establish two derived classes.

The three classes of Figure 7.2 form a hierarchy.

```
STUDENT -> HIGH_SCHOOL_STUDENT
STUDENT -> COLLEGE_STUDENT
```

The hierarchy means one class is derived from another class. We generally see a greater degree of specialization from the parent class to one of the derived classes. We can think of hierarchy as situations like

```
EMPLOYEE -> ADMINISTRATIVE_EMPLOYEE -> OFFICER
EMPLOYEE -> TECHNICAL_EMPLOYEE -> RESEARCHER
ALARM -> FIRE_ALARM
ALARM -> BURGLAR_ALARM
```

Figure 7.3 gives an example of three class definitions. The example is drawn from *Object-Oriented Programming Guide* for Turbo Pascal 5.5 produced by Borland International [Borland 1989]. This guide is an excellent introduction to object-oriented programming.

The first definition in Figure 7.3 is of a class called LOCATION. This is the base class of this series of definitions. The next class, called POINT, is derived from LOCATION. Points are defined as locations that can be made visible and moved. The class POINT inherits the instance variable x and y from the class LOCATION. It also inherits the procedure INIT and the functions XCOORD and YCOORD.

A third class, CIRCLE, is derived from POINT. This class is more sophisticated. Circles can be contracted or expanded, as well as moved. The three classes LOCATION, POINT, and CIRCLE form a hierarchy.

An issue that can be easily confused in object-oriented programing is the difference between inheritance and the use of another class within a class. Suppose we are defining a class called STUDENT. In order to define this class easily, we derive STUDENT from a class called PERSON. Thus, STUDENT inherits PERSON; a STUDENT is a subtype of the class PERSON. In defining the class STUDENT, we may also need to make use of another class called SOC_SEC_NUM to obtain and use social security numbers. The class STUDENT is *not* derived from SOC_SEC_NUM, but *uses* the class SOC_SEC_NUM just as one would use the class integer or the class string. This situation can be written as

```
STUDENT: class defined (PERSON)
uses SOC_SEC_NUM;
    . . .
```

There is also an important distinction to be made in the uses of inheritance. Inheritance can be used for two conceptually different purposes. These are subtyping and code reuse.

Subtyping is in some sense the natural use of inheritance. We have a class (for example, EMPLOYEE) that is already defined and has a certain set of operations. We wish to define a proper sub-class of this class (for example, ADMINISTRATIVE EMPLOYEE). See Figure 7.4.

The other use of inheritance is for the reuse of code. In this scenario, we have a class with a certain set of operations and we wish to introduce a class that has some similarities to one that is already defined. The existing class and the new class may not have any conceptual relation to each other. For example, we may have defined a class called PERSON and this class may have operations for reading a name, printing one's social security number, and recording one's date of birth. We may also be writing a card playing program and wish to define a class called PLAYER. We may not be interested in the date of birth of a PLAYER, but we might like to make use of input routines for reading the name of an individual. Such routines may perform error checking for appropriate format. In this instance, we might inherit the class PERSON simply to use some existing code.

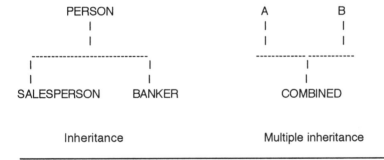

Figure 7.4 Inheritance vs. multiple inheritance.

Once we consider the idea of deriving one class from another we can readily move to a concept known as *multiple inheritance.* With multiple inheritance, a class is derived from more than one class. See Figure 7.4.

Thus inheritance means the ability to derive types based on previously defined types. Inheritance means that we can build on pieces that we already have. We can add new features or change particular features to get new abstractions. Inheritance means that we can use previously developed building blocks in creating new programs with different objectives and perhaps different properties.

7.3 POLYMORPHISM

As noted in [Raj et. al. 1991] and [Rao 1992] polymorphism falls into three categories.

1. *Ad hoc polymorphism.* This is essentially the same as overloading. That is, an operator or procedure works on arguments of different types. For instance, we may use the operator " <" to compare two integers or to compare two strings.

2. *Parametric polymorphism.* In this case, a definition has an explicit parameter to denote a type. Different versions of the definition are created when an actual type is provided. This is similar to the Ada facility for Generics, where, for instance, one might define a generic stack module and then instantiate it for a stack of integers or a stack of input transactions.

3. *Inclusion polymorphism.* This is the case where we have classes and subclasses. An operation or procedure applies to different elements of the classes and subclasses. A good example is the procedure DRAW to draw various kinds of shapes or objects.

It is the third kind of polymorphism that stems from inheritance.

Dynamic Binding

The degree to which an abstract data type or class can be extended is a central feature of object-oriented programming. With inheritance, we may have different derived types stemming from a given parent.

This, in turn, may mean that there are polymorphic procedures for which the actual types of the arguments may not be known until the time of execution. The ability to associate a specific procedure body at run time is called *dynamic binding*.

Consider Figure 7.3. In particular, consider the operation MOVE_TO given for the class circle. When this operation is invoked, the operation HIDE defined in the class CIRCLE will be invoked, then X and Y will be set to new values, and finally the operation SHOW for the class CIRCLE will be invoked. Notice that the definitions of HIDE and SHOW invoked by MOVE_TO are quite specific to the class CIRCLE.

Now notice that the operation MOVE_TO for CIRCLE is identical to the operation MOVE_TO for the class POINT. Suppose we deleted the operation MOVE_TO for CIRCLE. In this case, a call to MOVE_TO for an object of CIRCLE would implicitly invoke the operation MOVE_TO defined for POINT. At first glance, this might appear to be a simplification. There is, however, a difficulty. The operation MOVE_TO defined for POINT invokes the operations HIDE and SHOW defined for POINT. These operations do not give the correct meaning for hiding and showing a circle.

These apparent anomalies are a simple consequence of static binding, that is, the resolution of names by the compiler based on the information in the current scope. The example suggests that a different approach might be wise in conjunction with object-oriented programming. This gives rise to the phenomenon of *dynamic* binding.

Dynamic binding essentially means that the actual procedure invoked will not be determined until run time, when the types of arguments (which are polymorphic) are known. In such cases, the operation actually invoked will be the one defined for the arguments actually given. In Turbo Pascal, these operations are known as *virtual methods*. In C++, these are known as *virtual member functions*.

7.4   C++ AND ADA 95

C++

C++ is, of course, a major object-oriented language. Two of its design axioms are as follows:

1. A base of the programming language C.
2. A full and thoughtful implementation of object-oriented concepts.

The root of the object-oriented paradigm is the C++ construct for "class." In a simple form, a class appears as follows:

```
class PHONE_ENTRY {
   public:
   string LAST_NAME;
   string FIRST_NAME;
   string PHONE_NUM;
   void PRINT();
}

void PHONE_ENTRY::PRINT() { . . . }
```

A derived class can be defined as follows:

```
class FULL_PHONE_ENTRY: public PHONE_ENTRY {
   public:
   string STREET;
   string CITY_STATE;
   string ALTERNATE_PHONE;
   string NOTES;
   void PRINT();
}

void FULL_PHONE_ENTRY::PRINT() { . . . }
```

In C++, any initialization required for an object is handled by using constructors. A constructor can establish initial values or allocate space for an object. A constructor is automatically invoked when an object in the class is declared. In C++, more than one constructor can be defined; a particular constructor is chosen according to usual rules for overloading. Procedures called "destructors" can also be defined. A destructor is invoked when the scope of a declaration is exited.

C++ has many features that fully support the object-oriented paradigm. These include

Overloading of operators
Overloading of assignment
Dynamic binding
Constructors and destructors
Ability to define private information in classes

Appendix 2 contains a complete C++ program, which we discuss in the next chapter.

Ada 95

Ada takes a rather different approach to object-oriented methods. At the outset, the fundamental mechanism for encapsulation is the "package" rather than a "class." A package defines a collection of types, procedures, functions, constants, and variables; a class defines an abstract data type. Ada has no built-in mechanism for defining abstract data types. To get the effect of an abstract data type, the programmer needs to exercise special care to make sure things work as they should.

At a different level, Ada does not tackle design in the same way as "pure" object-oriented languages. In a superb article, Rosen [Rosen 1992] makes a number of points about Ada and object-oriented techniques. Rosen introduces the terms object orientation by classification and object orientation by composition. Classification is the use of abstract data types and inheritance, as in C++. Composition is the use of a set of parts to form an abstraction layer, as in Ada packages.

Ada, and here we specifically mean Ada 95, has features that provide substantial support for object-oriented programming. It allows a record type to be designated as "tagged." A "tagged" type in Ada 95 is a record type that can be modified with additional components. Tagged record types can be extended with new fields, and new procedures can be defined to operate over the extended type.

Although Ada does not have abstract data types as a language feature, Ada 95 does have all of the elements common to object-oriented programming. These elements include inheritance, polymorphism, and dynamic dispatching.

Consider the following:

```
-- (1)
type PHONE_ENTRY is tagged
   record
      LAST_NAME:   STRING(32)
      FIRST_NAME:  STRING(32)
      TELE_NUM:    STRING(16)
   end;
procedure PRINT (T: in PHONE_ENTRY);
```

We can extend the preceding with

```
-- (2)
type FULL_PHONE_ENTRY is new PHONE_ENTRY with
   record
      STREET:         STRING(32)
```

```
CITY:               STRING(32)
ALTERNATE_PHONE:    STRING(32);
NOTES:              STRING(64);
  end;
procedure PRINT(E: FULL_PHONE_ENTRY);
function ALTERNATE_PHONE_NUM(E: FULL_PHONE_ENTRY);
```

Here FULL_PHONE_ENTRY has seven fields, three of which are from the declaration of PHONE_ENTRY. The procedure PRINT is dispatching. The type PHONE_ENTRY'CLASS refers to an object that can be of type PHONE_ENTRY or of type FULL_PHONE_ENTRY.

If we declare

```
NEW_ENTRY:   PHONE_ENTRY'CLASS
```

then the call

```
PRINT(NEW_ENTRY);
```

will dispatch to the PRINT routine in (1) or (2), as determined by the actual value of NEW_ENTRY.

FURTHER READING

The textbook by [Deitel and Deitel 1994] is a superb introduction to C++.

A tutorial on object-oriented programming and its various technical aspects is given in [Rao 1992]. A detailed work on key specific issues in C++ is given in the work by Meyers [Meyers 1992]. A thorough treatment of C++, including a reference manual, is given in [Stroustrup 1991]. Bjarne Stroustrup is the designer of C++.

The use of inheritance is nicely cast in the Ada 95 Rationale [Ada Rationale 1993].

EXERCISES

Exercise 7.1 *Multiple Choice*

Pick the answer that best fits the question.

1. Three important concepts in OOP are
   a. syntax diagrams, inheritance, and structure.
   b. polymorphism, overloading, and structure.
   c. polymorphism, encapsulation, and inheritance.

    d.   structured programming, efficiency, and reliability.
    e.   parallelism, dynamic binding, and inheritance.

2.   Which of the following is the most accurate statement?
    a.   Inheritance is based on derived types.
    b.   Inheritance is based on polymorphism.
    c.   Inheritance is based on dynamic binding.
    d.   Inheritance is based on operator overloading.
    e.   Inheritance is based on using constructors.

3.   Which of the following languages supports overloading of assignment?
    a.   Fortran.
    b.   C.
    c.   Algol.
    d.   Pascal.
    e.   C++.

4.   C++
    a.   requires all type conversions to be explicit.
    b.   does not allow type conversions.
    c.   does not allow user-defined type conversions.
    d.   gives some legal interpretation to all use of types.
    e.   none of the above.

5.   In Mini-language Inherit,
    a.   Polymorphism is allowed.
    b.   Overloading of assignment is allowed.
    c.   Output of string variables is not allowed.
    d.   Constructors are not allowed.
    e.   Instance variables are not allowed.

6.   Which of the following constructs cannot occur in Mini-language Inherit?
    a.   `A := B or C;`
    b.   `while X loop Y.Z(); end loop;`
    c.   `while X loop Z(); end loop;`
    d.   `output Z.A(1);`
    e.   `Z := A + B + C;`

7.   Consider a class C that uses (not inherits) a class (or package) P.
    a.   The operations in P cannot be modified in C.
    b.   The visible names in C must be different from those in P.
    c.   C cannot be derived from another class.
    d.   C cannot make use of items declared in the implementation part of P.
    e.   All of the above.

Exercise 7.2 *Using Inheritance*

Using the syntax of Mini-language Inherit, write a small program that makes use of classes and inheritance. Choose a simple problem, as long as it makes some use of inheritance. You may add features to Mini-language Inherit to accommodate the problem you choose.

Exercise 7.3 *Bank Accounts*

Construct a description of three classes as follows:

a) The first class, called ACCOUNT, will include the basic functionality for a simple bank account. For example, it will have a balance, an owner, an owner's address, and so forth.

b) The second class, called CHECKING, will be derived from the class ACCOUNT. It will add some simple functionality for handling checks.

c) The third class, called SAVINGS, will also be derived from the class ACCOUNT. It will add some simple functionality for a saving account.

Give a complete description of the visible part of the three classes using the syntax of Mini-language Inherit. You may augment the syntax with additional constructs to include features not defined in the mini-language.

CHAPTER 8

Object–Oriented Programming

> *Designing good classes is hard because designing good types is hard*
>
> [Scott Meyers 1992]

 -oriented programming is not a simple matter to explain. In part, object-oriented programming is an attitude towards programming, a particular orientation. In part, it is also a particular style or philosophy. In part, it is also a terminology, a vocabulary.

We began our discussion of object-oriented programming with a chapter on data types and then presented a chapter about a follow-on topic, the definition of new data types. In a later pair of chapters, we discussed the idea of a module or a package and then considered the follow-on topic of objects and abstract data types. We then devoted a chapter to inheritance, a basic mechanism for deriving new classes of objects from existing classes.

8.1 WHAT IS AN "OBJECT"?

In our first mini-language, we discussed the concept of type. For example, we might declare a variable D as follows:

```
D: record
      YEAR:  integer;
      MONTH: integer;
      DAY:   integer;
   end;
```

With such a variable, we may freely update the components of D or refer to the components of D in an expression. This is elementary.

In Mini-language Typedef, we discussed the concept of type definitions. For instance, we might render the previous example in a better form as follows:

```
type DATE =
   record
      YEAR:  integer;
      MONTH: integer;
      DAY:   integer;
   end;
D: DATE;
```

Here we have defined a type called DATE and declared a variable D of type DATE. As before, we may freely refer to the fields of D. We could also write a procedure to print a date in some format or define an operator to add an integer number of days to a date.

If we wish to collect all the functionality of type DATE in one place, we could encapsulate the following:

```
ALL_ABOUT_DATES: module
   type DATE = record ... end;

   SET_DATE (integer, integer, integer) => DATE;
   YEAR(DATE)    => integer;
   MONTH(DATE)   => integer;
   DAY(DATE)     => integer;

   "+": (DATE, integer) => DATE;
   PRINT (DATE);
end;
```

In this case, we would have examples like

```
D:  DATE;
...
D := SET_DATE(1994, 7, 4);
PRINT (D)
```

This is the kind of abstraction given in Chapter 4 on Mini-language Modules.

We could make dates into full objects and have

```
DATE: type module
   SET_DATE (integer, integer, integer) => DATE;
```

```
   YEAR(DATE)     => integer
   MONTH(DATE)    => integer
   DAY(DATE)      => integer
   "+": (DATE, integer) => DATE;
   PRINT(DATE);
end;
```

as is done in Mini-language Objects. We would still write

```
D:  DATE;
...
D := SET_DATE(1994, 7, 4);
PRINT (D)
```

Here, however, the representation of a DATE is not directly available to a user.

Dates could next be abstracted as in Mini-language Classes:

```
DATE: class
   SET_DATE (integer, integer, integer) => DATE;
   YEAR()  => integer
   MONTH() => integer;
   DAY()   => integer

   "+": (DATE, integer) => DATE
   PRINT ( );
end;
```

In this mini-language, we make references like

```
D: DATE;
   ...
D.SET_DATE(1994,7,4);
D.PRINT();
```

We use the dot notation for functions and procedures that are applied to an object.

We also note that we could put the fields of a DATE directly in the visible part of a module. Thus, we could also have

```
DATE: class
   YEAR:  integer;
   MONTH: integer;
   DAY:   integer;
   PRINT();
end;
```

This is a fully valid example of Mini-language Inherit. In using this declaration, we may write

```
D:  DATE;
...
D.YEAR := 1994;
```

Here, given an object D of type DATE, we refer to the YEAR component of D with the notation D.YEAR.

In some renditions of object-oriented programming, we do not use the dot notation, but rather the more conventional listing of the object name as one of the arguments, as is done in Mini-language Modules.

There are different ways of defining an object, and the conventions used vary according to the particular programming language. The exact kind of abstraction we wish to make also depends upon the application at hand and one's individual judgment.

8.2 VARIETY OF OBJECTS

Returning back to one of the themes of this text, object-oriented programming is very much about nouns or things. In the previous examples for dates, it is easy for us to imagine programming-language constructs corresponding to a date, because a date is indeed a noun in ordinary discourse. One of the challenges of object-oriented programming, indeed one of the aspects that makes using object-oriented programming difficult, is viewing the programming world in this way. It is often difficult to imagine what kind of abstractions might be suitable in order to make the solution object-oriented. In some cases, this may take considerable time and energy, and one may not always succeed.

Consider the program of Figure 8.1. This example is due to [Chen 1993]. Here we describe an object called BUTTON. There is no direct representation of its "contents." The visible part of the type module defines only a single procedure (PUSH) and a single function (STATE). Nevertheless, this is an "object," a "noun." There is some kind of implicit storage for the object, the internal variable STATUS. Thus, we have an object whose visible interface is described only by giving the definition of two operations (PUSH and STATE).

Consider next the simple problem of writing a program to input two numbers and give the user a choice of whether to add, subtract, multiply, or divide these numbers. The program would thus act as a very simple

```
BUTTON: class
   procedure PUSH;
   integer function STATE(B: BUTTON);

implementation
   --0 means button is up (or off); 1 means down (or on);
   STATUS: integer;

   procedure PUSH is begin
      if (STATUS = 0)
         STATUS := 1;
      else
         STATUS := 0;
   end;

   integer function STATE(B: BUTTON) is begin
      return STATUS;
   end;
begin
   STATUS := 0;
end;
```

Figure 8.1   A push button Object.

calculator. We could write this program as a single main procedure, which prompts for input, selects the appropriate action, and prints the results.

How could we think of this elementary problem in term of objects? Consider the example of Figures 8.2 and 8.3. This example is due to [Smaili 1993]. In Figure 8.2, we have a class of objects called CALCULATOR. The class CALCULATOR is defined by five procedures, one to enter the x and Y values, the other four to perform the arithmetic. We could write a simple main program to use the CALCULATOR, as given in Figure 8.3.

The class module and main program are longer than we would have had by conventional, nonobject-oriented means. Nevertheless, the object-oriented solution is suggestive of general solutions where an object is defined by a collection of procedures.

This brings up the issue of what really can be represented as an "object." [Stroustrup 1991] enumerates a variety of possible classes, and based on his suggestions (page 403), we give the following list:

a)   basic data types (e.g., integer)

b)   related data types (e.g., long integer)

```
class CALCULATOR is

    procedure ENTER_XY;
    procedure ADD_XY;
    procedure SUBTRACT_XY;
    procedure MULTIPLY_XY;
    procedure DIVIDE_XY;

implementation
    X,Y: integer;

    procedure ENTER_XY is
    begin
        output "Enter two integers."
        input X,Y;
    end;

    procedure ADD_XY is
    begin
        output X, " + ", Y, " = ", X+Y;
    end;

    procedure SUBTRACT_XY is
    begin
        output X, " - ", Y, " = ", X-Y;
    end;

    procedure MULTIPLY_XY is
    begin
        output X, " * ", Y, " = ", X*Y;
    end;

    procedure DIVIDE_XY is
    begin
        output X, " / " Y, " = ", X div Y;
    end;
end;
```

Figure 8.2 A calculator.

```
program CALCULATE is
   C: CALCULATOR;
   CHOICE:  integer;
begin
   C.ENTER_XY;
   output "Enter 1,    2,        3,        or 4"
            "for   ADD, SUBTRACT, MULTIPLY, or DIVIDE";
   input CHOICE;

   if       (CHOICE = 1) ADD_XY;
   else if (CHOICE = 2) SUBTRACT_XY;
   else if (CHOICE = 3) MULTIPLY_XY;
   else if (CHOICE = 4) DIVIDE_XY;
   else output "No Cigar.";
end;
```

Figure 8.3   A program using the calculator.

c) basic higher-order types (e.g., lists, stacks, queues)

d) user-level types (e.g., days of the week)

e) user-level concepts (e.g., bank accounts)

f) generalizations (e.g., person, vehicle)

g) system resources (e.g., output streams, memory, disk drives)

h) higher-level concepts (e.g., supervisors, control units)

There certainly are more.

8.3   QUESTIONING OOP

We take note here of a rather fundamental issue raised in [Rosen 1992].
Object-oriented software is predicated on the notion of abstract data types
as forming a foundation for software development. With inheritance, the
abstract data types are developed in a hierarchy. Certain types in the
hierarchy draw attributes or properties from other types in the hierarchy.
Rosen calls this "Object Orientation by Classification First," or simply
classification. We can see this approach in examples like Employee -
Administrative Employee.

We can contrast this method with another approach, which Rosen calls "Object Orientation by Composition First," or *composition*. In the composition approach, we develop packages of constants, types, and procedures (not necessarily abstract data types). This approach is basically the approach taken in the original design of [Ada 1983] and is exemplified in Mini-language Modules given earlier. In this approach, we put collections of items together (constants, types, and procedures) that may be about a single data type, but more generally about a related collection of items. For instance, we may have a package comprising a number of input routines or output routines.

Rosen raises several questions:

- How relevant is object orientation by classification?
- Is object orientation by composition more useful?
- Is inheritance really useful?
- Can inheritance lead to problems?

Consider the program of Figure 7.3. Upon second thought, it is not at all clear that a *point* is a class derived from a *location*, nor is it at all clear that a *circle* is a class derived from a *point*. Although inheritance works technically in this case, and although the example well illustrates the use of inheritance, it is not clear how beneficial the solution is.

Again, as brought out by Rosen, inheritance itself brings some problems. To understand the behavior of the functions associated with a given class, one may have to inspect the true meaning of a parent class in order to understand the behavior of the inherited properties. The semantics of a class is thus not visible at a single level. This can introduce a hidden complexity that can grow over time.

8.4 PROGRAM FLASH

We next consider a somewhat larger program. The program is a simple monitor for a simple card game. The card game is called Flash. This card game was developed during one of the classes taught by one of the authors of this book (see [Jennings 1992] and [Survey 1992]). The game Flash is truly simple. There are two players. Each player begins by putting an amount of money in a pot. Each player is then dealt five cards. A player then chooses the maximum card in the hand. The player with the higher maximum card is the winner of the game and claims the money in the pot. (*Note*: One could add a round of betting after seeing one's cards. This would make the game much more interesting, but is not done here.)

A simple session might run as given in Figure 8.4. Here the players enter their names and initial amounts of money, and then a series of games is played. For each game, the program prints the two hands and the name of the winner.

A procedure-oriented solution to Flash is shown in Figure 8.5. This program follows the general Pascal style, where typically one gathers type declarations in one section, declares the procedures and functions next, and finally gives a main program. As mentioned before, there are many, many possible solutions to Flash and many different general styles.

You might imagine many programs for this game. For example, you might represent a deck of cards as an array of integers indexed from 1 to 52. This representation may not be the best when comparing two cards. For example, is card 46 greater than card 35?

Programming in an object-oriented manner means looking at a problem

```
Welcome to Flash
    Enter name for Player 1: Smith
    Enter money for Player 1: 45
    Enter name for Player 2: Jones
    Enter money for Player 2: 35

Game 1
Deal
    Smith: Hand is 4C JC 8H 5S QS
    Jones: Hand is AD 2H 9H 10S JS
Winner is Jones
Another game? Y

Game 2
Deal
    Smith: Hand is 6C 6D JH QH 7S
    Jones: Hand is 5C 6C 7D 2H KH
Winner is Smith
Another game? Y

    ...
```

Figure 8.4 A scenario for flash.

```
program FLASH is
   const
      HAND_SIZE = 5;
      ...
   type
      SUIT_NAME = (CLUBS, DIAMONDS, HEARTS, SPADES);
      RANK_VALUE = 2..14;
      CARD = record
                  SUIT: SUIT_NAME;
                  RANK: RANK_VALUE;
             end
      FLASH_HAND = array [1..5]  of CARD;
      CARD_DECK  = array [1..52] of CARD;
   ...
var
   COUNT: integer;
   SEED:  real;
...
procedure RANDOM (R: ref REAL) is
   ...
end;

procedure SET_UP_PLAYERS(P1, P2: ref PLAYER) is
   ...
end;

procedure NEW_DECK(D: ref CARD_DECK) is
   ...
end;

procedure DEAL_CARD(D: ref CARD_DECK; C: ref CARD) is
   ...
end;

function MAX_CARD(H: FLASH_HAND) return CARD is
   ...
end;
...
begin
   ...  { Main program }
end
```

Figure 8.5 A procedure-oriented program.

with a careful and well-tuned eye to discerning individual classes of objects. This is not an easy task. It takes time, effort, patience, and skill. We present a version of Flash that we believe is truly object-oriented. This is due in large part to [Jennings 1992] and is given in Figure 8.6.

Consider, for example, the class CARD. The type itself is represented internally by two instance variables. There is one operation, ">", for comparing the values of the cards. This is a kind of miniature implementation of a class of objects denoting the individual cards in a card deck.

The program Flash has a high degree of the object-oriented approach. It takes time to develop such abstractions. The benefit in doing so is quite far-reaching. In the first place, the main program evokes the true domain of cards, betting, and players. The reader of the program can relate to the problem domain rather than the domain of the programming language or the domain of the computer. The program reads in a natural fashion.

Moreover, the potential for extending the abstractions in Flash to include other card games is quite rich. One can imagine developing the classes, putting them into a library, and using them as a basis for card playing programs.

The program in Figure 8.6 contains only a small use of inheritance. It is worth reviewing even this small example. A PERSON is defined as an object containing two fields, a name and a social security number. A PLAYER, in turn, is derived from a PERSON. A PLAYER, however, adds the fields of an amount of money and a card hand. These are the features of a person who becomes a card player.

Flash in C++

Appendix B contains a solution to Flash in C++. It follows the solution given in this chapter and should be reasonably clear. The following points are relevant:

a) The symbol & denotes a "reference" to an object and is used for passing parameters by location. Thus PLAYER& denotes a "reference to PLAYER."

b) The string "\n" causes printing to advance to the next line.

c) The assignment operator "=" in the class MONEY_AMT is overloaded. This overloading allows assignment of integers and values of type MONEY_AMT to variables of type MONEY.AMT.

d) Overloading a binary operator in a class requires only specification of the second argument. The first argument is taken as a member of the class. A "friend" function or operator, on the other hand, can have arguments of any type and thus two are specified, as is done in the mini-languages. The assignment operator "=" cannot be defined as a friend.

e) In the main program, the file player.h is included with a #include directive. This file, in turn, includes `money_amt.h` and `flash_hand.h`. The file `flash_hand.h` includes `card_deck.h`, which in turn includes `card.h`. Thus all the header files are visible to the main program.

The solution to Flash in C++ fully supports separate compilation of classes, and separate compilation of the implementation parts for a class. As indicated above, we can imagine such classes forming a library of reusable software.

Glossary

Appendix C gives a glossary of terms. These terms summarize the key concepts in our presentation of object-oriented programming.

Figure 8.6 An object-oriented program.

```
program FLASH is
uses CARD, CARD_DECK, FLASH_HAND, MONEY_AMT, PLAYER;

    P1, P2:        PLAYER;
    HAND1, HAND2:  FLASH_HAND;
    C,
    MAX_CARD1,
    MAX_CARD2:     CARD;
    DECK:          CARD_DECK;
    ANTE, POT:     MONEY_AMT;
    COUNT:         integer;
    GAME_OVER:     boolean;

procedure SET_UP_PLAYERS (P1, P2: ref PLAYER) is
begin
    output "Enter name for Player 1: ";
    input    P1.NAME;
    output "Enter money for Player 1: ";
    P1.ENTER_MONEY();
    output "Enter name for Player 2: ";
    input    P2.NAME;
    output "Enter money for Player 2: ";
    P2.ENTER_MONEY();
end;

procedure ASK_ANOTHER_GAME (DONE: ref boolean) is
    RESPONSE: string;
begin
    output "Another game? ";
    input RESPONSE;
    if (RESPONSE = "y" or RESPONSE = "yes"
    or  RESPONSE = "Y" or RESPONSE = "YES")
       DONE := true;
    else
       DONE := false;
end;
```

Figure 8.6 (continued)

```
begin
    POT   := 0;
    ANTE  := 1;
    COUNT := 0;
    GAME_OVER := false;
    SET_UP_PLAYERS (P1, P2);
    DECK.NEW_DECK();

    while (not GAME_OVER) and (P1.MONEY > ANTE)
    and (P2.MONEY > ANTE) loop
        COUNT := COUNT + 1;
        output "\n";  output "Game ", COUNT;
        P1.MONEY := P1.MONEY - ANTE;
        P2.MONEY := P2.MONEY - ANTE;
        P1.HAND.CLEAR();
        P2.HAND.CLEAR();
        POT := ANTE + ANTE;

        DECK.SHUFFLE();
        output "Deal", "\n";
        for I := 1 to 5 loop
            DECK.DEAL_CARD(C);
            P1.HAND := P1.HAND + C;
            DECK.DEAL_CARD(C);
            P2.HAND := P2.HAND + C;
        end loop ;
        output P1.NAME, ": Hand is "; P1.HAND.PRINT();
        output "\n";
        output P2.NAME, ": Hand is "; P2.HAND.PRINT();
        output "\n";

        if (P1.HAND.MAX_CARD > P2.HAND.MAX_CARD) {
            P1.MONEY := P1.MONEY + POT;
            output "Winner is ", P1.NAME, "\n"; }
        else {
            P2.MONEY := P2.MONEY + POT;
            output "Winner is ", P2.NAME, "\n"; }
        POT := 0;
        ASK_ANOTHER_GAME (GAME_OVER);
    end loop ;
    output "The game is over.";
end;
```

Figure 8.6   (continued)

```
CARD: class
  LOW_CARD: constant CARD;
  >:      (CARD, CARD) => boolean;
  NEXT:  ( ) => CARD;
  PRINT: ( );

implementation
  type SUIT_NAME  = (CLUBS, DIAMONDS, HEARTS, SPADES);
  type RANK_VALUE = integer range 2..14;
  SUIT: SUIT_NAME;
  RANK: RANK_VALUE;

  operator > (CARD1, CARD2: CARD) => boolean is
    RESULT:   boolean;
  begin
    if (CARD1.RANK > CARD2.RANK)
       RESULT := true;
    else
       if ((CARD1.RANK = CARD2.RANK)
       and (CARD1.SUIT > CARD2.SUIT))
          RESULT := false;
       else
          RESULT := false;
    return RESULT;
  end;

  function NEXT() = > CARD is
    NEXT_CARD: CARD;
  begin
    if (RANK < 14) {
       NEXT_CARD.RANK := RANK + 1;
       NEXT_CARD.SUIT := SUIT;+ 1}
    else {
       NEXT_CARD.RANK := 1;
       NEXT_CARD.SUIT := SUIT.SUCC(); }
    return NEXT_CARD;
  end;
```

Figure 8.6   (continued)

```
procedure PRINT() is begin
    if      (RANK =  2) - 1 output "2";
    else if (RANK =  3) - 1 output "3";
       ...
    else if (RANK = 13) - 1 output "K";
    else if (RANK = 14) - 1 output "A";

    if      (SUIT = CLUBS)    output "C";
    else if (SUIT = DIAMONDS) output "D";
    else if (SUIT = HEARTS)   output "H";
    else if ((SUIT = SPADES)  output "S";
end;

begin
    LOW_CARD.RANK := 2;
    LOW_CARD.SUIT := CLUBS;
end;
```

Figure 8.6   (continued)

```
CARD_DECK: class
uses CARD;
   NEW_DECK:   ( );
   SHUFFLE:    ( );
   DEAL_CARD: (C: ref CARD);

implementation
   DECK_SIZE: integer;
   DECK: array [1..52] of CARD;

   procedure SWAP (C1, C2: ref CARD) is
      TEMP: CARD;
   begin
      TEMP := C1;
      C1   := C2;
      C1   := TEMP;
   end;

   procedure NEW_DECK () is
      C: CARD;
      I: INTEGER;
   begin
      C:= LOW_CARD;
      DECK[1] := C;
      for I := 2 to 52 loop
         C := C.NEXT;
         DECK[I] := C;
      end loop ;
      DECK_SIZE := 52;
   end;

   procedure SHUFFLE () is
      I, J, WIDTH: integer;
   begin
      for I := 1 to 51 loop
         WIDTH := 52 - I + 1;
         GET_RANDOM (WIDTH, J);
         SWAP (DECK[I], DECK[I + J]);
      end loop;
   end;
```

Figure 8.6   (continued)

```
procedure DEAL_CARD (C: ref CARD) is
begin
   C := DECK[DECK_SIZE];
   DECK_SIZE := DECK_SIZE - 1;
end;
end;
```

Figure 8.6   (continued)

```
FLASH_HAND: class;
   uses CARD, CARD_DECK;
   HAND_SIZE: constant integer := 5;
   "+":        (FLASH_HAND, CARD) => FLASH_HAND;
   MAX_CARD:   ( ) => CARD;
   CLEAR:      ( );
   PRINT:      ( );

implementation
   NUM_CARDS: integer;
   HAND:      array [1..HAND_SIZE] of CARD;

   procedure ADD_CARD (C: CARD) is begin
      NUM_CARDS := NUM_CARDS + 1;
      HAND[NUM_CARDS] := C;
   end;

   operator +:(H: FLASH_HAND; C: CARD) is begin
      H.ADD_CARD(C);
   end;

   function MAX_CARD: (HAND: FLASH_HAND) => CARD is
      I: integer;
      RESULT: CARD;
   begin
      RESULT := LOW_CARD;
      for I := 1 to HAND_SIZE loop
         if (HAND[I] > RESULT)
            RESULT := HAND[I];
      end loop;
      -- RESULT := the biggest card;
      return  RESULT;
   end;

   procedure CLEAR () is begin
      NUM_CARDS := 0;
   end;
```

Figure 8.6 (continued)

```
procedure PRINT () is
   I: integer;
begin
   for I := 1 .. HAND_SIZE loop
      HAND[I].PRINT();  output " ";
   end loop;
end;

begin
   NUM_CARDS := 0;
end;
```

Figure 8.6   (continued)

```
MONEY_AMT: class;
    +: (MONEY_AMT, MONEY_AMT) => MONEY_AMT;
    -: (MONEY_AMT, MONEY_AMT) => MONEY_AMT;
    <: (MONEY_AMT, MONEY_AMT) => boolean;
    >: (MONEY_AMT, MONEY_AMT) => boolean;
    ENTER_MONEY: ( );
    PRINT:      ( );

implementation
    VALUE:  integer;

    operator + (M1, M2: MONEY_AMT) => MONEY_AMT;
        M: MONEY_AMT;
    begin
        M.VALUE := M1.VALUE + M2.VALUE;
        return M;
    end;

    operator - (M1, M2: MONEY_AMT) => MONEY_AMT;
        M: MONEY_AMT;
    begin
        M.VALUE := M1.VALUE - M2.VALUE;
        return M;
    end;

    operator < (M1, M2: MONEY_AMT) => boolean is begin
        if (M1.VALUE < M2.VALUE)  return true;
        else                      return false;
    end;

    operator > (M1, M2: MONEY_AMT) => boolean is begin
        if (M1.VALUE > M2.VALUE)  return true;
        else                      return false;
    end;

    procedure ENTER_MONEY ( ) is begin
        input VALUE;
    end;

    procedure PRINT ( ) is begin
        output VALUE;
    end;
end;
```

Figure 8.6 (continued)

```
PERSON: class
   NAME:     string;
   SS_NUM:  string;
end;

PLAYER: class derived(PERSON)
uses FLASH_HAND;
   HAND:  FLASH_HAND;
   MONEY: MONEY_AMT;
   ENTER_MONEY: ( );

implementation
   procedure ENTER_MONEY () is
      VALUE: MONEY_AMT;
   begin
      input VALUE;
      MONEY := VALUE;
   end;
end;
```

APPENDIX A

General Exercises

A.1 *Multiple Choice*

Pick the answer that best fits the question.

1. Which of the following is not a programming language?
   a. Algol 67.
   b. Simula 67.
   c. Concurrent C.
   d. Objective C.
   e. Turbo C.

2. Which of the following terms is not particularly related to object-oriented programming?
   a. Global variable.
   b. Instance variable.
   c. Simula 67.
   d. Smalltalk.
   e. Operator overloading.

3. In OOP, the dot notation is often used for
   a. procedure calls.
   b. string variables.
   c. type declarations.
   d. operator definitions.
   e. dynamic binding.

4. Which of the following is most related to object-oriented programming?
   a. Top–down programming.
   b. Structured programming.
   c. Modular programming.
   d. Logic programming.
   e. Real-time programming.

5. Which of the following is most related to object-oriented programming?
    a. Top–down programming.
    b. Structured programming.
    c. Modular programming.
    d. Logic programming.
    e. Real-time programming.

6. In informal terms, "object-oriented" means
    a. basing design on data types rather than on procedures.
    b. putting declarations into classes.
    c. hiding the representation of data.
    d. programming without global variables.
    e. using the techniques of structured programming.

A.2   Fill in the Blanks

Use the following list of terms to fill in the blanks below. Use the term that best fits the situation and use each term only once.

Class	Abstract Data Type
Constructor	Member Function
Encapsulation	Dynamic Binding
Inheritance	Instance Variable
Type	Overloading
Flash	Polymorphism

a. A situation that results because of inheritance and polymorphism.
    _____

b. Can be used to modify a previously defined class.
    _____

c. Type + Encapsulation = _____

d. Part of the public interface of a class. _____

e. A popular card game. _____

f. Can be used to allocate space for an object. _____

g. An Ada package exemplifies this. _____

h.   Part of the state of an object. _____

i.   Private types are used for this. _____

j.   A basis for object-oriented programming. _____

A.3   *The J. P. Rosen Quiz*

This quiz is based on the article "What Orientation Should Ada Objects Take," by J. P. Rosen, *Communications of the ACM,* November 1992 [Rosen 1992]. The task is to read this paper and answer the following questions.

Part (a) *Multiple Choice*

Pick the answer that best fits the question.

1.   Ada is not fully object-oriented because
    a.   the language does not allow polymorphism.
    b.   the language does not support data hiding.
    c.   there is no way to define parameterized types.
    d.   the encapsulation mechanism (packages) is not based on objects.

2.   According to Rosen, object orientation by *classification* is
    a.   the organization of data into distinct types.
    b.   the partitioning of algorithms into distinct procedures.
    c.   the use of a hierarchy of classes.
    d.   a method of structuring based on dynamic binding.

3.   According to Rosen, object-orientation by *composition* is
    a.   the organization of data into distinct types.
    b.   an assembly of lower-level components.
    c.   the use of a hierarchy of classes.
    d.   a method of structuring based on dynamic binding.

4.   According to Rosen, proponents of OOP make this fallacious argument:
    a.   We generally think of objects as being organized into classes.
    b.   The procedures operating on data should be defined with the data.
    c.   Encapsulation is an important part of programming.
    d.   Software design should be supported by specific methods.

5. Consider the following:

```
type POINT is record
    X: integer;
    Y: integer;
end;
```

to declare a point on a screen. There is a problem here in that
a. a point is not a type.
b. X and Y should not be of type integer.
c. a record type should not be used.
d. polymorphism.
e. none of the above.

6. Which of the following features is the most central to both the classification approach and the composition approach to object orientation?
a. Encapsulation.
b. Polymorphism.
c. Inheritance.
d. Abstract data types.
e. Data hiding.

7. Consider the following:

```
class Complex {
    double  r, i;
public:
    Complex {double x = 0, double y = 0)  {r = x; i = y; }
    double re()  {return r; }
    double im()  {return i; }
    void operator+= (Complex z) ...
    void operator-= (Complex z) ...
    void operator*= (Complex z) ...
    void operator/= (Complex z) ...
}
```

This is an example of
a. abstract data types.
b. inheritance.
c. composition.
d. global variables.
e. dynamic binding.

8. In contrasting Ada and C++,
    a. Ada "with" clauses are non-transitive.
    b. in C++, inheritance is transitive.
    c. redefining assignment for a class redefines assignment for all derived classes.
    d. all of the above.
    e. none of the above.

9. In Ada 95, a tagged type
    a. allows for type extension.
    b. allows for inheritance.
    c. allows for dynamic binding.
    d. all of the above.
    e. none of the above.

10. According to Rosen, a serious issue with the classification approach is that
    a. it is not a valid scientific approach.
    b. it is not clear that it applies to software development.
    c. inheritance is difficult to follow.
    d. inheritance is difficult to implement.
    e. all of the above.

Part (b) *Short Answer Quiz*

Prepare a written answer of about a half page to each of the following:

1. What is the definition of "polymorphism" given in the paper?

2. Give three reasons found in the paper in favor of inheritance.

3. Give three reasons found in the paper against inheritance.

A.4   *The Flash Quiz*

Multiple Choice. With regard to program Flash of Figure 8.6, pick the answer that best fits the following questions.

1. In the main program,
    a. all the cards are dealt to one player before the next player receives a card.
    b. a new deck of cards is established for each game.
    c. the amount of money owned by a player is checked to see if it is sufficient to cover the betting in a game.
    d. the social security number of each player is printed.
    e. the cards are shuffled once every 10 games.

2. The variable C in the main program
    a. is a local counter.
    b. represents a deck of cards.
    c. holds the value of a single card.
    d. is used to print an output value.
    e. denotes the winning card in the two hands.

3. In the class CARD,
    a. the type SUIT_NAME is hidden from users of the class.
    b. PRINT prints the rank and suit of a card.
    c. the operator "<" is not defined for two cards.
    d. LOW_CARD denotes the lowest card in the deck.
    e. all of the above.

4. In the class FLASH_HAND,
    a. the class MONEY is used for local variables.
    b. PRINT prints the size of a hand.
    c. the operator "+" is defined for two cards.
    d. LOW_CARD holds the current lowest card in a hand.
    e. ADD_CARD adds a given card to a hand.

5. In the procedure ENTER_MONEY defined for the class PLAYER,
    a. values like 1,000 (with commas) are allowed as input.
    b. values like $38 (with dollar signs) are allowed as input.
    c. negative values are allowed as input.
    d. the procedure ENTER_MONEY for the class MONEY_AMT is called.
    e. a limit is placed on the amount of money a player can use.

A.5   Modifications to Flash in C++

It can be very instructive to modify a program. The following is a list of modifications to the program of Appendix 2. Each modification serves a noble purpose. With all modifications, demonstrate that the corrections work.

(a)   Minor Corrections

The following is a list of minor problems that would be good to fix in the program.

1. Add the operators ">=" and "<=" to class MONEY_AMT.

2. Check that the name entered for a player at least begins with a letter.

3. Modify Flash so that hands are cleared after the game (as is done in real card games), not before (as is done in the current version).

Make the corrections.

(b)   *Class Boolean*

In Appendix 2, the type boolean is simulated using integers and the #define directive. Add a class called boolean that simulates the type boolean and include operators for logical "and," "or," and "not."

(c)   *Accepting Money Literals*

It would be good to accept money amounts such as

$12   12,000 $12,000

an input. Thus, we could have

    Enter money amount for Player 1: *$42*

Modify class MONEY_AMT to accept as input money amounts with $'s and commas.

(d)   *Overloading the Output Operator "<<"*

The program of Appendix 2 does not allow output of cards using the "<<" operator. Thus,

    cout << "Max card is" << C;

where C is of class CARD is illegal. Modify the class CARD to allow cards to be output using "<<".

(e)   *Betting in the Middle*

Flash actually becomes interesting as a betting game if each player is allowed to bet after seeing one's cards. The opponent's cards must be kept blind. The game then is like five-card poker.

Modify the program of Appendix 2 to prompt for a round of betting after the cards are dealt. Give each player a chance to raise the bets on a second round of betting.

(f)   *A Game Supervisor*

It is possible to simplify the main program for Flash by adding a new object. One possible object is a game monitor or game supervisor. Another possibility is an input-output interface. Either construct such an object for addition to the program or prepare a one- or two-page paper on the difficulties of this issue.

APPENDIX B

Flash Source Code in C++

```
//  Standard libraries, Classes
#include <iostream.h>
#include <string.h>
#include "player.h"

//  Definitions
#define false 0
#define true  1
#define boolean int

// -- Program FLASH
main (void)
{
    PLAYER      P1, P2;
    FLASH_HAND  HAND1, HAND2;
    CARD        C, MAX_CARD1, MAX_CARD2;
    CARD_DECK   DECK;
    MONEY_AMT   ANTE, POT;
    int         COUNT;
    boolean     ANOTHER_GAME;
    void SET_UP_PLAYERS (PLAYER&, PLAYER&);
    void ASK_ANOTHER_GAME (boolean&);

// -- Main program
    POT   = 0;
    ANTE  = 1;
    COUNT = 0;
    ANOTHER_GAME = true;
    SET_UP_PLAYERS (P1, P2);
    DECK.NEW_DECK();
```

```
while ((ANOTHER_GAME == true) && (P1.MONEY > ANTE)
&& (P2.MONEY > ANTE)) {
   COUNT =  COUNT + 1;
   cout << "\n";
   cout << "Game " << COUNT << "\n";
   P1.MONEY = P1.MONEY - ANTE;
   P2.MONEY = P2.MONEY - ANTE;
   P1.HAND.CLEAR();
   P2.HAND.CLEAR();
   POT = ANTE + ANTE;

   DECK.SHUFFLE();
   cout << "Deal" << "\n";
   for ( int I = 1; I <= 5; ++I) {
      DECK.DEAL_CARD(C);
      P1.HAND = P1.HAND + C;
      DECK.DEAL_CARD(C);
      P2.HAND = P2.HAND + C;
   }
   cout << P1.NAME << ": Hand is ";  P1.HAND.PRINT();
   cout << "\n";
   cout << P2.NAME << ": Hand is ";  P2.HAND.PRINT();
   cout << "\n";

   if (P1.HAND.MAX_CARD() > P2.HAND.MAX_CARD()) {
      P1.MONEY = P1.MONEY + POT;
      cout << "Winner is " << P1.NAME << "\n"; }
   else {
      P2.MONEY = P2.MONEY + POT;
      cout << "Winner is " << P2.NAME << "\n"; }
   POT = 0;
   ASK_ANOTHER_GAME (ANOTHER_GAME);
}
cout << "The game is over." << "\n";
}
```

```
void SET_UP_PLAYERS (PLAYER& P1, PLAYER& P2)
{  cout << "Enter name for Player 1: ";
   cin  >>  P1.NAME;
   cout << "Enter money for Player 1: ";
   P1.ENTER_MONEY();
   cout << "Enter name for Player 2: ";
   cin  >>  P2.NAME;
   cout << "Enter money for Player 2: ";
   P2.ENTER_MONEY();
}


void ASK_ANOTHER_GAME (boolean& OK) {
   char  RESPONSE[12];

   cout << "Another game? ";
   cin  >> RESPONSE;
   if (strcmp(RESPONSE,"y")==0 || strcmp(RESPONSE,"yes")==0
   || strcmp(RESPONSE,"Y")==0 || strcmp(RESPONSE,"YES")==0)
     OK = true;
   else
     OK = false;
}
```

```
// file card.h
#define false 0
#define true  1
#define boolean int

class CARD {
   public:
      friend boolean operator > (CARD, CARD);
      const CARD  LOW_CARD();
      CARD        NEXT();
      void        PRINT();

   private:
      enum SUIT_NAME {CLUBS, DIAMONDS, HEARTS, SPADES};
      typedef int RANK_VALUE;   // range 2..14
      SUIT_NAME   SUIT;
      RANK_VALUE  RANK;
};
```

```
// file card.c
#include "card.h"
#include <iostream.h>

boolean operator > (CARD CARD1, CARD CARD2) {
   boolean RESULT;
   if (CARD1.RANK > CARD2.RANK)
      RESULT = true;
   else
      if  ((CARD1.RANK == CARD2.RANK)
      &&   (CARD1.SUIT > CARD2.SUIT))
         RESULT = true;
      else
         RESULT = false;
   return RESULT;
}

CARD CARD::LOW_CARD() {
   CARD C;
   C.RANK = 2;
   C.SUIT = CLUBS;
   return C;
}
```

```
CARD CARD::NEXT() {
    CARD NEXT_CARD;

    if (RANK < 14) {
        NEXT_CARD.RANK = RANK + 1;
        NEXT_CARD.SUIT = SUIT; }
    else {
        NEXT_CARD.RANK = 2;
        NEXT_CARD.SUIT = SUIT + 1; }
    return NEXT_CARD;
}

void CARD::PRINT() {
    if       (RANK == 2)  cout << "2";
    else if (RANK == 3)  cout << "3";
    else if (RANK == 4)  cout << "4";
    else if (RANK == 5)  cout << "5";
    else if (RANK == 6)  cout << "6";
    else if (RANK == 7)  cout << "7";
    else if (RANK == 8)  cout << "8";
    else if (RANK == 9)  cout << "9";
    else if (RANK == 10) cout << "10";
    else if (RANK == 11) cout << "J";
    else if (RANK == 12) cout << "Q";
    else if (RANK == 13) cout << "K";
    else                 cout << "A";

    if       (SUIT == CLUBS)    cout << "C";
    else if (SUIT == DIAMONDS) cout << "D";
    else if (SUIT == HEARTS)   cout << "H";
    else                       cout << "S";
}
```

```
// file card_deck.h
#include "card.h"

class CARD_DECK {
   public:
      void NEW_DECK();
      void SHUFFLE();
      void DEAL_CARD(CARD&);
   private:
      int  DECK_SIZE;
      CARD DECK[52];
      void SWAP (CARD&, CARD&);
};



// file card_deck.c
#include "card_deck.h"
#include <stdlib.h>
extern "C" int rand();

void CARD_DECK::SWAP (CARD& C1, CARD& C2) {
   CARD TEMP;
   TEMP = C1;
   C1   = C2;
   C2   = TEMP;
}

void CARD_DECK::NEW_DECK() {
   CARD C;
   int I;
   C = C.LOW_CARD();
   DECK[0] = C;
   for (I = 1;  I < 52; ++I) {
      C = C.NEXT();
      DECK[I] = C;
   };
   DECK_SIZE = 52;
}
```

```
void CARD_DECK::SHUFFLE() {
   int I, RAND_POS, WIDTH;

   for (I = 0;  I < 52; ++I) {
      WIDTH = 52 - I;
      RAND_POS = I + rand()%WIDTH ;
      SWAP(DECK[I], DECK[RAND_POS]);
   }
}

void CARD_DECK::DEAL_CARD(CARD& C) {

   C = DECK[DECK_SIZE - 1];
   DECK_SIZE = DECK_SIZE - 1;
}
```

```
// file flash_hand.h
#include "card_deck.h"

class FLASH_HAND {
   public:
      const int HAND_SIZE = 5;
      FLASH_HAND();
      friend FLASH_HAND operator + (FLASH_HAND, CARD);
      CARD    MAX_CARD();
      void    CLEAR();
      void    PRINT();
   private:
      int     NUM_CARDS;
      CARD    HAND[HAND_SIZE];
      void    ADD_CARD(CARD);
};



// file flash_hand.c
#include "flash_hand.h"
#include <iostream.h>

FLASH_HAND::FLASH_HAND() { NUM_CARDS = 0;}

void FLASH_HAND::ADD_CARD(CARD C) {
   NUM_CARDS = NUM_CARDS + 1;
   HAND[NUM_CARDS - 1] = C;
}

FLASH_HAND operator + (FLASH_HAND H, CARD C) {
   H.ADD_CARD(C);
   return H;
}

CARD FLASH_HAND::MAX_CARD() {
   int I;
   CARD RESULT;

   RESULT = RESULT.LOW_CARD();
   for (I = 0;  I < HAND_SIZE; ++I) {
      if (HAND[I] > RESULT)
         RESULT = HAND[I];
   };
```

```
      // RESULT = the biggest card;
      return RESULT;
}

void  FLASH_HAND::CLEAR() { NUM_CARDS = 0;}

void FLASH_HAND::PRINT() {
   int I;

   for (I = 0;   I < HAND_SIZE; ++I) {
      HAND[I].PRINT();
      cout << " ";
   }
}
```

```
// file money_amt.h
#define false 0
#define true  1
#define boolean int

class MONEY_AMT {
    public:
        friend MONEY_AMT operator + (MONEY_AMT, MONEY_AMT);
        friend MONEY_AMT operator - (MONEY_AMT, MONEY_AMT);
        friend boolean operator < (MONEY_AMT, MONEY_AMT);
        friend boolean operator > (MONEY_AMT, MONEY_AMT);
        MONEY_AMT& operator = (int&);
        MONEY_AMT& operator = (MONEY_AMT&);
        void ENTER_MONEY();
        void PRINT();
    private:
        int VALUE;
};


// file money_amt.c
#include "money_amt.h"
#include <iostream.h>

MONEY_AMT operator + (MONEY_AMT M1, MONEY_AMT M2) {
    MONEY_AMT  M;
    M.VALUE = M1.VALUE + M2.VALUE;
    return M;
}
MONEY_AMT operator - (MONEY_AMT M1, MONEY_AMT M2) {
    MONEY_AMT  M;
    M.VALUE = M1.VALUE - M2.VALUE;
    return M;
}

boolean operator < (MONEY_AMT M1, MONEY_AMT M2) {
    if (M1.VALUE < M2.VALUE)  return true;
    else                      return false;
}
boolean operator > (MONEY_AMT M1, MONEY_AMT M2) {
    if (M1.VALUE > M2.VALUE)  return true;
    else                      return false;
}
```

```
MONEY_AMT& MONEY_AMT::operator = (int& I) {
   VALUE = I;
   return *this;
}

MONEY_AMT& MONEY_AMT::operator = (MONEY_AMT& M) {
   VALUE = M.VALUE;
   return *this;
}

void MONEY_AMT::ENTER_MONEY() {
   cin >> VALUE;
}

void MONEY_AMT::PRINT() {
   cout << "$" << VALUE;
}
```

```
// file player.h
#include "flash_hand.h"
#include "money_amt.h"

class PERSON {
   public:
      char  NAME[20];
      char  SS_NUM[20];
};
class PLAYER: public PERSON {
   public:
      FLASH_HAND  HAND;
      MONEY_AMT    MONEY;
      void ENTER_MONEY();
};


// file player.c
#include "player.h"

void PLAYER::ENTER_MONEY() {
   MONEY_AMT M;
   M.ENTER_MONEY();
   MONEY = M;
}
```

APPENDIX C

Glossary

Abstract Data Type	A type whose representation is not available to the user.
Abstraction	Hiding of details that do not contribute to essential characteristics.
Class	An abstract data type. A programming language construct similar to modules where the module itself is the type.
Composite Type	A type whose objects have multiple parts (e.g., an Account may have a name, balance, ID, . . .).
Constructor	A procedure that initializes an object (e.g., by setting a local state or allocating storage).
Dynamic Binding	Association of a specific item (e.g., a specific procedure body) at run time. Needed if resolution is not resolvable at compile time.
Encapsulation	Grouping of essential characteristics (e.g., all about commands or all about telephone numbers).
Hierarchy	A tree-like collection of types.
Information Hiding	Putting an object variable inside the implementation part of a module.
Inheritance	Ability to derive types based on previously defined types. Operations on the parent type apply to a derived type.
Instance	An object (i.e., a member of a class).
Instance Variable	A variable that is defined within a module defining a class. The variable is part of the internal state of the object.

Member Function	A procedure or function defined as one of the operations for a type.
Message	Procedure call applied to an object. The procedure is one of the member functions defined with the object (or higher in the object hierarchy).
Multiple Inheritance	Ability to derive types based on several parent types.
Object-Oriented	A perspective of classes and things (i.e., objects or nouns).
Overloading	The ability to use the same procedure name or operator with different types of arguments.
Polymorphism	The ability to use the same procedure name or operator with different types of arguments. The term has an implication that the different types form a hierarchy.
Process	An object that is a task.
State	An object may have a "state," a set of local variables with individual values (e.g., an Account may have name, balance, ID, . . .).
Type	A set of objects and the operations on the objects.
Type Manager	A module that contains a type definition and operations. The module itself is not the type.

References

[Ada 83]
Reference Manual for the Ada Programming Language,
U.S. Department of Defense, Washington, 1983 (also published by Springer-Verlag, New York, 1983)

[Ada 95]
Ada 95 Reference Manual
Intermetrics Inc., Cambridge, MA, 1995

[Ada Rationale 95]
Ada 95 Rationale
Intermetrics Inc., Cambridge, MA, 1995

[Allen and Cocke 1972]   Frances E. Allen and John Cocke
"A catalogue of optimizing transformations,"
In *Design and Optimization of Compilers,* Randall Rustin, Editor,
Prentice Hall, Englewood Cliffs, NJ, 1972

[Borland 1989]
Object-Oriented Programming Guide, for Turbo Pascal 5.5
Borland International, Scotts Valley, CA, 1989

[Booch 1991]   Grady Booch
Object-Oriented Design, with Applications
Benjamin Cummings, Redwood City, CA, 1991

[Brosgol 1977]
"Is Ada Object-Oriented?"
In *Alsy News,* Alsys Inc., Burlington, MA, 1977

[C]   Brian W. Kernighan and Dennis M. Ritchie
The C Programming Language
Prentice Hall, Englewood Cliffs, NJ, 1978

[Chen 1993] Yin Chen
Unpublished Push-Button program
Prepared for course CSE 408, Survey of Programming Languages,
University of Toledo, Fall 1993

[Cleaveland 1986]   J. Craig Cleaveland
An Introduction to Data Types
Addison-Wesley, Reading, MA, 1986

[Croy 1993]   Kelly Croy
Unpublished Class-Student program
Prepared for course CSE 408, Survey of Programming Languages,
University of Toledo, Fall 1993

[Deitel and Deitel 1994]   H. M. Deitel and P. J. Deitel
C++ How to Program
Prentice Hall, Englewood Cliffs, NJ, 1994

[Dersham and Jipping 1990]   Herbert L. Dersham and Michael J. Jipping
Programming Languages, Structures and Models
Wadsworth, Belmont, CA, 1990

[Eiffel]   Bertrand Meyer
Eiffel: The Language
Prentice Hall, Englewood Cliffs, NJ, 1992

[Gries and Gehani 1977]   David Gries and Narain Gehani
"Some ideas on data types in high-level languages"
Communications of the ACM, vol. 20, no. 6, June 1977, pp. 414–420

[Guttag 1977]   John V. Guttag
"Abstract data types and the development of data structures"
Communications of the ACM, vol. 20, no. 6, June 1977, pp. 396–404

[Guttag and Horning 1978]   John V. Guttag and James J. Horning
"The algebraic specification of abstract data types"
Acta Informatica, vol. 10, 1978, pp. 27-52

[Hoare 1969]   C.A.R. Hoare
"An axiomatic approach to computer programming"
Communications of the ACM, vol. 12, no. 10, October 1969, pp. 576–580

[Hoare 1973]   C. A. R. Hoare
"Hints on Programming Language Design"
(In *Computer Systems Reliability,* Infotech State of the Art Report no. 20, Infotech, Maidenhead, England, 1974)

[Ichbiah *et al.* 1979]   Jean Ichbiah *et al.*
"Rationale for the design of the Ada programming language"
Sigplan Notices, vol. 14, no. 6, Part B, June 1979

[Jennings 1992]   Marko Jennings
Unpublished notes on "Flash," an object-oriented card game
Prepared for course CSE 408, Survey of Programming Languages, Computer Science and Engineering Department, University of Toledo, Fall 1992

[King 1991]   Joe King
"A beginner's guide to OOP: Object oriented programming"
Computers in Education Division of ASEE

[Ledgard 1971]   Henry F. Ledgard
"Ten Mini-Languages: A study of topical issues in programming languages"
ACM Computing Surveys, vol. 3, no. 3, September 1971, pp. 115–146

[Liskov and Zilles 1974]   Barbara H. Liskov and Stephen N. Zilles
"Programming with abstract data types"
Sigplan Notices, vol. 9, no. 4, April 1974, pp. 50-59

[Marcotty and Ledgard 1986]   Michael Marcotty and Henry F. Ledgard
Programming Language Landscape, 2nd Ed.
Science Research Associates (SRA), Chicago, IL, 1986

[Meyers 1992]   Scott Meyers
Effective C++ , 50 Specific Ways to Improve Your Programs and Designs
Addison-Wesley, Reading, MA, 1992

[Modula-2]   Niklaus Wirth
Programming in Modula-2, 2nd Ed.
Springer-Verlag, New York, 1983

[Morris 1973]   James H. Morris
"Types are not sets"
Proceedings of Sigplan/Sigact Symposium on the Principles of Programming Languages, Boston, October 1973, pp. 120–124

[Parnas 1971]   David L. Parnas
"Information distribution aspects of design methodology"
Proceedings of the 1971 IFIP Congress
North Holland Publishing Company, Amsterdam, 1971, pp. 339–344

[*Raj 1991*]   Rajendra K. Raj, Ewan Tempero, and Henry M. Levy
"Emerald: A general-purpose programming language"
Software Practice and Experience, vol. 21, no. 1, January 1991

[Rao 1992]   Bindu R. Rao
C++ and the OOP Paradigm
CAP Gemini America Series
McGraw-Hill, New York, 1992

[Rentsch 1982]   Rentsch
"Object-Oriented Programming"
Sigplan Notices, September 1982

[Rosen 1992]   J. P. Rosen
"What orientation should Ada objects take?"
Communications of the ACM , vol 35, no.11, November 1992

[Sebesta 1993]   Robert W. Sebesta
Concepts of Programming Languages
Benjamin/Cummings, Redwood City, CA, 1993

[Seidewitz 1991]   Ed Seidewitz
"Object-Oriented Programming with Mixins in Ada"
Technical Report, Goddard Space Flight Center, Greenbelt, MD, 1991

[Sethi 1989]   Ravi Sethi
Programming Languages-Concepts and Constructs
Addison-Wesley, Reading, MA, 1989

[Simula 67]   Ole-Johan Dahl, B. Myhrhaug, and U. Nygaard
The Simula 67 Common Base Language
Norwegian Computing Center, Oslo, 1968

[Smaili 1993]   Khalid Smaili
Unpublished Calculator program
Prepared for course CSE 408, Survey of Programming Languages,
University of Toledo, Fall 1993

[Smalltalk]   Adele Goldberg and David Robson
Smalltalk-80: The Language and Its Implementation
Addison-Wesley, Reading, MA, 1983

[Stansifer 1995]   Ryan Stansifer
The Study of Programming Languages
Prentice Hall, Englewood Cliffs, NJ, 1995

[Strachey 1967]   Christopher Strachey
Fundamental Concepts in Programming Languages
International Summer School in Computer Programming, Copenhagen,
1967

[Stroustrup 1988]   Bjarne Stroustrup
What Is Object-Oriented Programming
IEEE Software, May 1988 (1991 revised version, AT&T)

[Stroustrup 1991]   Bjarne Stroustrup
The C++ Programming Language, 2nd Ed.
Addison-Wesley, Reading, MA, 1991

[Survey 1992]
"Object Oriented Programming: A Polymorphic Overview "
Class notes prepared by students in the CSE 408, Survey of High-Level
Languages class, University of Toledo, Fall 1992. Students were Tod
Cunningham, Sameer Gupta, Marko Jennings, Sumanth Madimsetty,
Ronald Mazur, and Khaled Saleh.

[Survey 1993]
Student example programs, prepared by students in the CSE 408, Survey of High-Level Languages class, Computer Science and Engineering Department, University of Toledo, Fall 1993. Students were Ying Chen, Kelly Croy, Roger Klenz, Mohammad Niazzi, Tom Owen, Khaled Smaili, Harold Steinmetz, and Craig Szczublewski.

[Wilson and Clark 1988]   L. B. Wilson and R. G. Clark
Comparative Programming Languages
Addison-Wesley, Wokingham, England, 1988

[Wirth 1983]   Niklaus Wirth
Programming in Modula-2, 2nd Ed.
Springer-Verlag, New York, 1983

Index